June 2007

AWA WITH WORDS

Young Writers' 16th Annual Poetry Competition

It is feeling and force of imagination that make us eloquent.

How can I not dream while writing? The blank page gives a right to dream.

YoungWriters

Scottish Verses

Edited by Heather Killingray

 Young**Writers**

First published in Great Britain in 2007 by:
Young Writers
Remus House
Coltsfoot Drive
Peterborough
PE2 9JX
Telephone: 01733 890066
Website: www.youngwriters.co.uk

SB ISBN 978-1 84431 115 6

Foreword

This year, the Young Writers' *Away With Words* competition proudly presents a showcase of the best poetic talent selected from thousands of up-and-coming writers nationwide.

Young Writers was established in 1991 to promote the reading and writing of poetry within schools and to the young of today. Our books nurture and inspire confidence in the ability of young writers and provide a snapshot of poems written in schools and at home by budding poets of the future.

The thought, effort, imagination and hard work put into each poem impressed us all and the task of selecting poems was a difficult but nevertheless enjoyable experience.

We hope you are as pleased as we are with the final selection and that you and your family continue to be entertained with *Away With Words Scottish Verses* for many years to come.

Contents

Robert Gordon's College, Aberdeen

Rudolf Steiner School, Edinburgh

St Ninian's High School, Glasgow

St Thomas Aquinas RC Secondary School, Glasgow

The Poems

Goodbye

She was always quiet,
Hiding something,
She was in her own world,
Hiding from something,
She'd go out by herself,
In her black coat,
She'd go out, her hood up,
Hiding her face,
She was by herself a lot,
In her room,
She would sit on her bed,
Her coat beside her,
She made a decision,
That coat beside her,
She left that night,
The darkness surrounding her,
She turned back,
Saw me at my window,
She wasn't wearing her coat,
Had left it on her bed,
She had left it for me,
To remember her by,
She looked straight at me
And she smiled through her tears,
She was crying as she waved,
Waved me goodbye.

Louise Brown (14)
Mackie Academy, Stonehaven

The Doomed Organ

The kingly organ will play no more
For its home is doomed to rot.
Its slender pipes have no one to play for
The church's congregation has lost the plot.
I and my sister, sitting at the back
Wonder why we are the only children there.
The old congregation, led by Jack
Follow the Father's Holy Prayer.
They fail to notice the dwindling
Of the size of the congregation.
The church is meant to be a place of love
And a place of wonderful sensation,
So now the organ shall play no low or shrill
Beautiful music from upon the hill.

Chris Horn (14)
Mackie Academy, Stonehaven

The Lamp Post

Tall and silent by the road,
A stark sentinel, standing alone,
Cold and bare in the morning light.

People passing by without a thought,
Or scratching life and death upon its sides;
The clumsy love and loss of teenage strife.

Still it stands, humming low and soft,
Oblivious to the bustle down below,
A pointless metal pole, or so it seems.

But as the day comes to a close
And shadows lengthen over darkened streets,
The lamp post brings light to the world.

Sam Dickinson (14)
Mackie Academy, Stonehaven

Lonely Sanctuary

It's quiet.
Alone up here,
Peaceful, tranquil.
Here, I'm alone,
Alone with my thoughts
And none are the wiser.
Sometimes . . .
It is pleasant
To be by oneself.
The wind blows through my hair,
The rock at my back,
This place is my haven.
To be alone by the sea,
Away from the hectic bustle.
I wish it was real
But it isn't, I'm afraid,
That I'm the only one who comes here.
I'm safe,
Alone
In my mind.

Sarah Woodfin (15)
Mackie Academy, Stonehaven

Pen

The most powerful weapon in the world
The power to give life
Or take it away with a simple hand movement
It can officialise the adjoining of a couple
Or announce their split
It can bring peace or declare a war
It can break any barrier
The pen is forever.

Isla MacLean (15)
Mackie Academy, Stonehaven

Last Day On Earth

There's a slight chill in the air as I step out the back door
The apocalypse is today . . .
I pull my coat up to hide my neck from the gentle breeze
I guess it is colder than I thought.
The apocalypse is today . . .
Walking down the road I see faces
I do not know them
They do not know me.
The apocalypse is today . . .
I steer towards the hill
I climb the path.
The apocalypse is today . . .
I reach the top
The memorial stands before me
It is beautiful in the rising sun
The sun will not reach full rise.
The apocalypse is today . . .
The sea stretches out in front
To the right and to the left.
The apocalypse is today . . .
I look over the town
I see many people
They are smiling
They are laughing
They do not know.
The apocalypse is today . . .
I will miss this place
These people
A bird passes in front of the sun.
The apocalypse is today . . .
I look out at the horizon
I can see it already
It will reach us soon.
The apocalypse is today . . .
People are all around me now
They know too
I only see one face I recognise

He waves to me
We are in line now
Holding hands
Facing the sea.
The apocalypse is today . . .
It reaches us
I breathe in my last breath
And close my eyes
So do the people whose hands I hold beside me
Around me
There is no fear.

Only love.

The apocalypse . . . *was* today.

Katie Bell (14)
Mackie Academy, Stonehaven

Cold Winter Nights

The winter family guardian
On the cold winter nights
Keeps the family close
But instigates the fights

Everybody wants to be closest
The youngest always wins
If it weren't for the stove
We wouldn't wear a grin

Jack Frost would come through the windows
And seep into our lungs
Especially with the laminate floor
We will get numb bums

If it wasn't for our trusted stove
Our winters would be nightmares!

Robert Davies (14)
Mackie Academy, Stonehaven

Seasons Of Companionship

Alone and forlorn it lies
In the cupboard with the pet food, discarded,
As useless, no longer needed.
A glimpse of it reminds me
Of long summer days, spent lying
On the beach, dog at my feet.
Of her, running and tumbling
Through long grasses, down steep hills.
Its scent brings forward in my mind
Chill winter mornings, by the fire
Curled up, her warmth against me.
Her, fighting through snow
White flakes on her nose and covering her fur.
Flecks of dirt and small black hairs;
Bringing back the first time I saw this puppy
Smaller than my own foot,
Helpless, yet so full of life.
This tiny, grimy collar, discarded
By the dog food, so full
Of memories, treasured forever,
Of my dog, my best friend,
Companion through the seasons,
Friends throughout the years.

Jennifer Keenan (14)
Mackie Academy, Stonehaven

The Plane

The long white wings,
On the short, boxy fuselage
White with anger!
The engine roars
And away it goes
Up, up, up
Further and further
Still it's going up
I can't stop it
It stops sharply
And starts coming down
Faster and faster
I can't control it
Oh no! *Smash!*
It crashes into the ground
The long white wings
Broken in two
The short, boxy fuselage
Flat
That is why
The plane was white with anger.

Glen Moir (14)
Mackie Academy, Stonehaven

Winter

Winter's eve,
When the tall oak groans and
Northern winds howl,
When cruel frost creeps silently,
White,
Beneath the bark,
And twigs, once soft and green,
Whisper and sway in the darkness.

Inside, flames crackle in the hearth,
Sending dancing shadows through the
Darkness.
I grasp my blanket tighter as rain batters against the windowpane
And skeleton branches
Patter gently,
On the slates above.

Charlotte Eggo (12)
Mearns Academy, Laurencekirk

Be My Valentine

Love is like a red, red nose
On a winter's day
Or like pink tulips
In the middle of May.

These scenes describe how I feel about you
You always make me feel brand new
I'm so happy since we met
Let us try, I'll make a bet.

But this is just my imagination
My happiness, joy and feeling of elation
Is just another dream
Things just aren't what they seem.

Lynsey Cathro (13)
Monifieth High School, Monifieth

What If . . .

What if you were a bird,
Flying so high,
Freedom is not just a word,
When you're soaring in the sky.

What if you could be jelly,
Any colour that you wish,
But you would go into someone's belly,
After being served on a dish.

What if you were the ocean,
Going backwards and forwards all day,
Would you lose your emotions,
On the sandy bay?

What if you could be a tree,
Home and shelter for any animal,
You wouldn't be free,
When you're highly inflammable.

What if you were a day,
Gone in twenty-four hours,
There are thirty-one in May,
Everything could change, like flowers.

I'm just Joanne Smith,
With a big imagination,
I love December the 24th
And this is one of my creations.

Joanne Smith (13)
Monifieth High School, Monifieth

Close Down

The secret life in your soul,
Is hidden to all but you,
You never show that side of you,
To yourself be true.

You've lost those people,
Who care for you most,
Stop yourself from fading away,
Stop being a ghost.

When you look in the mirror,
Do you see what I see?
Do you recognise what you've lost
And what you could be?

What has made the change in you?
Please let me be included,
You have only yourself to blame,
Stop being so deluded.

Calum Dwyer (15)
Monifieth High School, Monifieth

You

You're the person who made me laugh
You're the person who made me cry
You're the person who made me hurt inside

You're the person who held my hand
You're the person who hugged me
You're the person who made me believe

You're the person who promised me you'd be there
You're the person who said, 'I love you'
You're the person who lied.

Hannah Taylor (15)
Monifieth High School, Monifieth

Me And My Dog

I look in her eyes,
Her brown dull eyes.
I kiss her nose,
Her silky wet nose.

I feel she is mine
And no one else's.
As she is my precious,
Like my little girl.

She is very small,
But with a heart of gold.
She loves to be loved,
As well as her own space.

When we walk in the park,
She chases all the birds.
She loves me lots
And I love her back.

Cara Snowball (14)
Nairn Academy, Nairn

School Dinners

School dinners
Death on a plate
Catch me eating them
You won't!
For I much prefer
The crispiness of a sausage roll
A MacLean's baguette? A salad perhaps?
Doughnuts, pastries, éclairs, pies and sweets
It's my seventh heaven
It's what makes my heart beat
A bag of chips?
Maybe I say
I can have some another day.

Sean Henderson (14)
Nairn Academy, Nairn

Torn Apart

All these nightmares flying through my head
The bittersweet smell of blood just shed
Oh, how I long to be safely home in my bed
Instead of here, surrounded by the nightmares I dread.

All I can see with these strange new eyes
They feel like my own, but they feel like they lie
Across the way, my brother's deep sigh, but why?
Should I really be here or am I meant to die?

The burning new pain that I now feel
Only with sweet fresh blood shall it heal
To these vampire eyes, my brother's life shall be my first meal
By his side I move to and kneel.

I cannot do this, I shall resist, I must
I would sooner face the sun and turn to dust
Rather than betray a lifetime of dear Riku's trust
Even if I'm damned to the underworld, beneath the Earth's crust.

I try to rise, but once more I fall
Leaving me with no other choice, but to crawl
I go to confront whatever fate is mine to befall
At the hand of this vampire, the one they call Squall.

Gemma Innes (14)
Nairn Academy, Nairn

A Poem About Life

(Dedicated to Daniel Burgess, a good friend, he will be sadly missed)

Life is precious
More precious than the sun
More precious than the stars
More precious than time itself

Yet every day at least ten lives are wasted
All for the sake of making one
Life is heard all around the country
All over the world even, possibly in space

Life is heard on the news
Yet it still hurts when
Death knocks on your door
Life is precious

Life competes with death
Yet death continues to win
Life is nothing but a miracle
Death is nothing but pain.

Tony Doyle (14)
Nairn Academy, Nairn

The Whitewash

As Brett Lee ran up the side of the wicket
Andrew Flintoff was deciding where to hit it.
The wickets were falling in such a flurry
That Andrew Flintoff was caught in the gully.
Ricky Ponting was not sorry!
As Adam Gilchrist was Viv Richards' worry!
As Kevin Pietersen dropped the catch
Michael Vaughan saw The Ashes falling into the hatch.
Shane Warne made his 700 mark
As England were way off the mark.

Patrick Gerring (14)
Nairn Academy, Nairn

Freedom

Freedom itself is a wonderful thing
The flowers, the birds and how they sing
Freedom itself rules us all
But the amount of freedom is very small.

For you see, we are trapped
In darkness and gloom
To this we must adapt
To relieve us from eternal doom.

All I want is freedom
Is that too much to ask?
All I want is freedom
To forget my horrible past.

Freedom from war
Freedom from death
Freedom gives sight
Freedom gives breath.

Cry freedom
With a bold voice
Cry freedom
And *rejoice!*

Amy Cameron (14)
Nairn Academy, Nairn

Grandad

Here's a tribute to my grandad
He was a very special man
He loved a little whiskey
And a song and dance

He joined the Royal Navy
And sailed the seven seas
Then, he met my granny
And life was such a breeze

After he married
He became an ice cream man
He loved to scoot about the town
In his little ice cream van

Then he had six children
Who all grew up so fast
Then he had six grandchildren
And life was such a blast

He never saw them grow
Because he had to pass
So this is why I write this poem
To make his memory last.

Stevie Martin (13)
Perth Academy, Perth

I Ran, I Ran

I ran, I ran
Away from everything
My life, my soul, my heart
I couldn't take anymore
So I shut the door
And decided to make a fresh start
So I ran, I ran

I ran, I ran
Up a hillside
And gazed up into the night
And as I lay down
On the soft grassy ground
I dreamt of a wonderful sight
Where I'd ran, I'd ran

I ran, I ran
Through a meadow
With a beautiful yellow painted sky
Where the flowers were blooming
And nothing was stirring
And peacefulness flashed in my eyes
So I ran, I ran

I ran, I ran
Through that magical meadow
Where I thought life was never hard
But I tripped and I fell
And I never could tell
What had happened, as I woke with a start
And I ran, I ran

I ran, I ran, I'd ran, I'd ran
I ran, I ran, back home.

Claire Addison
Perth Academy, Perth

Imagine

Imagine a rainbow without the colours,
Dull, boring and grey,
Imagine a flower without its petals,
It shouldn't be that way.
Imagine a book without any words,
Just blank, empty pages,
Imagine a zoo without any animals,
Just empty, quiet cages.
Imagine music without any sound,
Just empty, silent staves,
Imagine the sea without any movement,
No clear blue crashing waves.
Imagine a candle without any flame,
No warm flicker of light,
Imagine the sky without any stars,
Just a dark, dreary night.
Imagine a necklace without any fasteners,
A useless string of beads,
Imagine a pond without any water,
Just a deep pit full of reeds.
Imagine the sun without its glow,
Only a dull circle in the sky,
Imagine the birds without any wings,
No flocks flying by.
Imagine Coke without any bubbles,
No fun, no zing, no fizz,
Imagine life without these things,
I like it the way it is.

Jane Byers (13)
Perth Academy, Perth

Men At War

The men at war,
The men at war,
The men at war,
Lie on the floor.

Fighting with guns,
Fighting for lives,
Fighting for a chance
To see their wives.

Once again
The troops are there,
Killing men
Who act like bears!

Whilst injured pass
Run for cover,
Most end up in hospital,
Some, but not others!

As the hospital
Runs out of beds
You can hear an explosion
Far ahead.

Hearing sirens,
Everyone panics,
Looking for their loved ones
As they scarper for cover.

The British troops
Run down to the dust,
Helping the Iraqis
But thrusting it back!

Please, please
Mr Bush and Blair,
Stop this war
And send them back!

Natalie Dormer (13)
Perth Academy, Perth

New York

New York with its bright lights
And its famous sights
The Empire State
It's first rate
Smoking sewer vents
Apartments to rent
Go for a spin around town
Or maybe just go downtown
FDNY saves the damsel in distress
NYPD go catch the rest
Brooklyn Bridge or Hunter's Ridge
Explore Little Italy
Or catch a boat out to Lady Liberty
Go to a Starbucks
Or feed Central Park ducks
Have a look round
Hear all those sirens sound
Bronx Zoo
Is that a film crew?
'Friends' coffee house
Look at the size of that mouse!
Ground Zero
The place of heroes
Heavy snow
Your car's being towed
Taxis of yellow
The drunk on the corner bellows
Broadway, wrong way
No place I'd rather be
New York is the place for me!

Scott Smith (13)
Perth Academy, Perth

The Race

All cars ready
The lights go down
The cars are steady
Go . . .
The cars are off
They travel fast
They race around the bends
Nobody wants to be last
That's one lap
Neck and neck
This is the most dangerous corner
Nobody wants to be another wreck
They are at the final bend
Racing down the straight
That's it, over
The red car has won
He will be back at another date.

Mark Scrimgeour (13)
Perth Academy, Perth

The Owl

A creature of darkness,
It swoops down on its prey,
It sees in the night,
As we see in the day,

He flies beneath a starry sky,
Above the trees,
But not too high,

As dawn approaches,
He returns home,
To sleep on a branch,
All day long.

Alison Suttie
Perth Academy, Perth

Paper Round

The alarm shrieks me awake!
Cocooned,
I know January's snow awaits me.
Stumbling into crumpled jeans,
Fumbling the lid off the toothpaste,
A zing of water kicks me in the face.
Creeping about cautiously,
But secretly tempted to stir those still sleeping,

Peeling back the door into the shredding blast,
Frozen fingers fiddling at the lock,
Climbing onto my bike as quick as an oak,
I struggle up the slope
And along the desolate streets.

Alone,
Out in the open,
Sleet drives downward like the bars of my cell.
Solitary confinement,
Imprisoned for a wage.

Chris Sneddon (14)
Perth Academy, Perth

My Shadow

I have a little shadow that goes everywhere with me,
He stays so close beside me, he's a coward for all to see.

The best thing about him is the way he likes to grow,
Not at all like us, which is very slow.

Sometimes he shoots up, taller than a man
And sometimes he gets so small; he's smaller than a can.

He follows me everywhere and follows me to bed,
He jumps in when I jump in and sleeps beside my ted.

Megan Elrick (13)
Perth Academy, Perth

Warfare

Warfare is a terrible thing,
Gone are the swords that went *cling,*
With guns and bullets,
Bombs and turrets
And soldiers who are fools,
The soldiers think they are bringing peace,
Woefully deceived are they,
War leads to war,
Invention after terrible invention,
Will it ever stop?
Nuclear and biological,
Everyone's health is endangered,
Iraq, Iran, Afghanistan,
Are we really any different?
East should leave the West alone
And the West should leave the East,
For everyone is a beast,
A world in harmony?
The idea seems barmy,
But if it were so,
We may all live and grow,
Contact between nations, yes,
But trade and tourism is a better way,
Guns and bullets have had their day!

Jonathan Jacobs (14)
Perth Academy, Perth

Ode To A Woodpecker

Your plumage is simply fit for kings,
With every feather perfect,
Right down to the chevrons under your tail,
Your every movement graceful.

You stand up proud atop your tree,
Knowing that everyone's jealous,
You descend to maybe halfway up
And start the samba rhythm.

Your signature is world renowned,
That *tap-tap* is so famous,
You have been made into a star,
Of everybody's forest.

You whistle, chirrup, sing and dance
And brighten up the pine trees,
But the only mansion you'll ever have,
Is one that's called a bird box.

Your wondrous cloak of black, white, red,
I'm sure is much sought after,
But want doesn't get and they will have,
To be satisfied with pictures.

Andrew Forbes (14)
Perth Academy, Perth

The Almost Tragic Journey

As the doors close and the engine starts,
We slowly make our way to depart,
The engines rattle and the seat shakes,
The wheels turn and we lurch forward,
We pull out of the drive
And down the road,
All squashed in with a tremendous load,
Then, in the city, the traffic is at a stand,
My dad then makes funny gestures with his hand.

We're now at the twisting country roads,
Tight turns ahead,
Our mango air freshener that hangs from the roof,
At a sharp turn, is gone in a poof.

We're on the main road now, freedom at last,
My dad takes this chance to go extra fast,
But no! Our fun soon comes to an end,
Because of a very silly man,
In a camper van!
As we try to pass the cathedral on wheels,
A mini kitchen and four tonnes of steel,
We pull out but notice a turn,
To overtake on the straights, my dad must learn,
For a car is coming up straight ahead,
Luckily though, they swerve into a hedge,
'Woohoo! On to Blackpool!' we shout,
So get ready England, you'd better watch out!

Ruairidh Horne (13)
Perth Academy, Perth

The Man With The Golden Finger

There once was a man with a golden finger,
He had no teeth and his hair was ginger,
He had huge lips and purple eyes,
He was incredibly fat and liked to eat pies,
He had six arms and a pointy beak,
He had no friends for he was a geek,
He had huge feet and bright green toes,
He had slimy toenails where fungi grows,
He had huge glasses and liked to do math,
He smelt really bad for he had never had a bath,
No one liked him and he came from Liverpool,
He thought he was cool, as he slavered and drooled,
He lived on a farm with his great auntie Kim,
Who unfortunately was as ugly as him,
They lived together in their old farmhouse shed,
They lived on fried rice and peed in their beds,
Apart from poor Kim, who couldn't pee
And this only added to her own misery,
A fairy once came and gave them a wish each,
She said you could wish for a house made of bleach!
The man wished to be handsome; a warrior with might,
Kim wished she could pee, to make everything alright,
Now the two live together, as happy as can be,
The man is handsome and Kim can pee!

Ross Nicoll (13)
Perth Academy, Perth

Free

It gives the illusion of going places
The letters came
Scattered the paratroopers
A change of continents
Who else has been here?
Where we think all the funny stuff goes on
And the day I left home
Cold and expired of home
I needed it for myself
To be free
Free from hesitation

Crouching in the long shrubs
There was a sudden bang
Then a thud
The flow of blood streamed out
Then someone smiled
I was going to be all right
Then I saw the light
I saw death
But death never came.

Michael Murphie (13)
Perth Academy, Perth

Greed

The sun sets on a winter's day,
The long, cold night begins
And, like our history, it's full of shadows,
Shadows created by ourselves,
War, famine, pestilence, death,
They stain our past,
It's what we're best at,
Destroying what is good for some petty gain,
It's our nature that needs to change,
If we're to turn our future into a summer's day.

Matt Munro
Perth Academy, Perth

The Weather

The summer sun shone brightly
Casting shadows down the road
The sunset fell softly
Leaving a warm glow

The rain poured down in sheets
Bouncing off the roads
Then the rain fell gently
Leaving puddles in potholes

The frost sparkled on the pavement
Across the frozen grounds
The pathways were slidy
As the ice glinted in the light

The wind came in gusts
Knocking over trees
Swirling like a hurricane
Then it fell to a breeze.

Rebecca Cantwell   (14)
Perth Academy, Perth

Rainbow

Rainbow in the sky so bright,
All colours there, black and white,
A pot of gold,
Lies at the end,
A dream come true,
It's all for you.

The storm has been,
A rainbow has arrived,
You'll get from this,
Whatever you derive.

With a rainbow around,
It's all great,
Is this really all just fate?

Elisa Kerr
Perth Academy, Perth

The Rainbow

They come out of work to crumpled grey skies,
Just as torn-faced as a child that cries.
They fight their way through bustling city crowds,
In their perfect suits with briefcases, just fake shrouds.

For deep within their secret soul,
There is a smile waiting to roll
And far above the drooping clouds
The sun is waiting to shine aloud.

But then the ocean droplets arrive,
Splashing and soaking cars and drives.
Washing away the city grime,
Making grass a luxurious lime.

The rain collects in gurgling drains,
The sloshing and slurping sounds seem to say,
'We've cleaned and now we flow away.'

As the water continuous to fall,
The bland black clouds shrink so small.
The falling droplets are into every place,
Making people shiver and brace.

People dislike the cruel, cold features of rain,
Such as numbing fingers and toes with slight pain.
Suddenly, the sun breaks free,
Warmth and light are spread with glee.

And as the rain drives defensively on,
The sun does too and brightly it shone.
And as the rain and sun blended,
They make a sight that is truly splendid.

Seven glorious colours shine blazingly through,
Spreading a smile to every person and their neighbour too.
A rainbow will always bring happiness
To no matter who.

Katie Smith (13)
Perth Academy, Perth

Hiding

I hide behind a perfect mask,
Down to earth and right on task.
I smile lightly when people are around,
But when they leave, I have a breakdown.

How many times do they expect me to forgive
And forget?

Why do they think I am hard-pressed
Forced into a smile and cheerful front?
I have to be strong, not let it out,
Never come close and never disclose.
Be strong as the sun and brave
As the fighter that I am.

Most will never go through what I have had
To endure.

Yet they expect me to be like an open door.

What do they think? I am some sort of fool
I am much wiser than most for my age
And no longer want to deal with the pain.

So, I stand just as strong as a battered stone
Chipped and bruised, yet confident
I will not love, I will not cry, I will not do anything
But deny -

I have not hope for this world.

Jade Sinclair
Perth Academy, Perth

A Misty Dawn To Dusk

With the easterly rising sun it approaches
Timed is the singing of the dawn chorus
The first shafts of light hit the sky
Pink, orange, golden beams shine above
But the scene is changing
A mist wanders up the river
Slowly, creeping forward
Lurking above the water
But soon the moment has passed, the light has gone
Consumed by the beast.

As it wanders, it slows
Soon it too will disappear with the day
Just as the light did
By the midday sun it is gone
Mysteriously vanished into the air
By the riverside it clears
No signs of its presence
But it will be back
Later.

The day is coming to an end
The sun begins to set
Once more something stirs by the riverside
Cautiously creeping, it advances
Once more consuming all in its path
It is wary but continues
Taking the evening with it
The day has passed
And the night has come
A storm is brewing on the horizon.

Fergus Gill (14)
Perth Academy, Perth

A Poem About Football

Football is the beautiful game,
Or that is how it's known
And that is the subject,
For this very poem.

The two teams play against each other,
With eleven on each side
And then there is the book of rules,
By which they must abide.

The whistle blows, the game begins,
Ninety minutes to go,
The play goes from end to end,
But then we score a goal.

Ten minutes later, the whistle goes
And the ref signals half-time,
As we jog towards our coach, he says,
'Lads, you're doing fine.'

The second half was same as the first,
But we scored two more goals
And when the final whistle blew,
The score was 3-2.

Both teams shook hands with each other
And congratulated them,
But as you know there's only one winner
And that was the best team on the day.

Alan Thom (14)
Perth Academy, Perth

Why Do You Label Me?

Emo, Mosher or Goth
Why does everyone have to have a group?
Labelled constantly
I want to be my own person, not like everyone else
Why can't they see I am my own person?

People say I cut myself 'cause of the way I dress
I don't, you can check my arms, belly and legs
But people can't see I'm not that kind of person
I am a happy person, I love a laugh
These people that label me
They see me laugh and fool about
But they have an image in their heads
And nothing can change that image
I don't understand
Why everyone needs to be labelled
I am my own person.

Jennie Reid
Perth Academy, Perth

It Hurt

It hurt inside for her,
These people had what she so desired,
Watching them, day to day,
It made her tired.
Soon, she wished, it would be her day,
Things may eventually go her way.
She gazed longingly at the boy
As a tear came to her eye,
She knew she could not have,
She would not try.
She'd have to settle for what she had,
With jealousy she thought she would go mad,
Her mouth would water as she pictured it in a dream . . .

If only there weren't so many calories in chocolate ice cream!

Kimberley White (14)
Perth Academy, Perth

The Abandoned Child

Why is this house so dark?
All that neighbour's dog is doing
Is *bark, bark, bark!*
When will they be back?
Why did she tell me to stay in my room?
It feels like a cold, wet tomb,
When should I go downstairs?
This is not fair,
Why don't they care?
That's it,
I am going down the broken stairs to sit,
The wallpaper has lots of tears,
But that is OK because I have my teddy bear,
My arms are all sore,
There are rips in the floor,
Now I feel sick,
This house is a tip,

When will they be back?
I will go outside,
I hope they don't mind?
When will they be back?
Don't they care?

Zara Khan (15)
Perth Academy, Perth

Grandma

It has been years now since you were gone,
The sadness still carries on,
How I miss you so,
In some ways, it was a blessing you had to go.

Your smile brought warmth in every soul,
The happiness made everyone feel whole,
You were so funny in your little ways,
'Oh, my hat!' you used to say.

I remember sitting in the garden with you,
Flowers blossomed in shades of pink, yellow and blue,
On all occasions you dressed to delight,
The jewellery you wore was a dazzling sight.

Even though you passed away,
In my heart is where you stay,
One thing which will last until the end,
Is the continuing love you send.

Yvonne Henderson (14)
Perth Academy, Perth

The Hunter

Can you see the kingly beast?
That precious jewel shining within the grassland deep
Its arrogance unrivalled in the animal order.

Can you see its inner strength?
Its majesty and natural stealth
It prowls with dignity, stalking its unknowing prey.

Can you search beyond its formidable glare?
And behold those eyes, those captivating eyes
With its stature, strong and bold.

Its prowess and almost perfect form
Intrigues our minds and invokes our fascination
And man must yield to its killer instincts when unleashed.

Lewis Richardson (13)
Robert Gordon's College, Aberdeen

Tarantula

In the warm evening of North American summer
Something stirs in the darkness!

Tarantula!
With its hairy legs and dark, beady eyes;
Tarantula!
With its grotesque hissing sound and dark, evil body;
Tarantula!

Suddenly, it turns towards me;
All eight beady eyes staring
And I am suddenly afraid.

Those dark eyes
And that dark, evil-looking body
Takes all hope away from me
And replaces it with fear . . .

And then, as I move, it hisses
And the hairs on my back stand
And my spine goes cold.

Then I am angry
How dare he come here!
How dare he come to my home . . .
And humble me!

So I strike it,
I strike it with a rock
And I watch it crawl back
I watch it crawl back into its hole.

Kyle Wong (12)
Robert Gordon's College, Aberdeen

The Frog

Fat, green, jolly and round,
A frog jumps past,
Boing!
Higher and higher the frog jumps.

It pauses for a moment and catches flies,
Ribbet!
Croak!
It jumps again.

It jumps higher and higher still,
Higher, higher, always higher, never stopping,
I wonder why it doesn't tire?
Higher and higher the frog bounces.

Ribbet! Ribbet!
The frog croaks, as if in victory,
Yet higher and higher it hops,
Never stopping, always hopping.

It stops, defeated at last,
The frog sits on a lily pad and rests,
It lies lazily as if nothing has happened
And waits to start again.

Rebecca Elder (13)
Robert Gordon's College, Aberdeen

Gibbon

Swinging from tree to tree, calling to his mate,
His yellow body flashes past,
He stops, he jumps up, he calls to his mate again,
It echoes, there is no reply.

Without warning, he leaps forward,
Swinging from tree to tree,
Calling to his mate,
His call echoes,
He becomes frantic.

Now, almost flying through the air, he continues to call,
His white face is etched with worry,
His body is tense,
Without her, he is nothing.

There is a call, he replies,
His yellow body flashes past,
He stops, he leaps down,
Lying on the floor he finds her,
Motionless,
He cries - it echoes.

Jess McClean (12)
Robert Gordon's College, Aberdeen

Lamb

What's that woolly bundle laying in the field there?
A little woolly bundle sleeping in the summer sun,
Tired out by its day of prancing, pouncing fun.

It lies so still in the warm summer sun
And what's that there lying with it?
A black bin liner? No . . .
A crow!
A villain of the skies,
Come down to dine of finest cuisine,
Lamb's eyes!

Away, away, you foul bird!
And back to its distant perch it flapped
There it sat and gazed down with its piercing glare
How dare it just sit there and stare
Not even thinking of the damage it's done!

The lamb just lay there,
Gaping holes where its eyes once shone from.
Never again would it prance and pounce
And forever now it will lie in the summer's sun.

Roddy Douglas (13)
Robert Gordon's College, Aberdeen

The Panther

Long, black sleek coat
Slinking through the jungle;
Black, soft paws
Padding along the jungle floor
The panther hunting for the hunted.

Suddenly!
A flash of black!
The panther strikes
And another victim falls prey
To the black, ferocious panther.

The panther stealthily drags
The dead, lifeless, carcass of a deer
To its hideaway layer
Beneath the big, moraceae tree,
Where it sleeps a peaceful
But ever-vigilant sleep.

And another day is done
For the ever-sly panther.

Ben Thomas (13)
Robert Gordon's College, Aberdeen

Tiger

I walked through the jungle.

Alone.

Something golden-brown
In the corner of my eye . . .

Tiger.

Its golden stripes shone
In the light.
It looked at me and stared,
Unblinking.

Its golden stare mesmerised
And I,
Entranced by its beauty,
Stood still.

I forgot completely that
In a matter of seconds
I could be dead.

Suddenly,
It moved.

Panic overcame me,
I gripped my Winchester tight.
Steady . . .
Aim . . .
Finger on the trigger now . . .
Wait!

I could not kill it now!
I could not end it all here!
I could not destroy that beauty!
It was not right!

I just could not do it!

I lowered the rifle.
The tiger stopped.
Stared.

Its eyes glinted at me,
Smiling.
I smiled back.

It turned.
Ran.
Back into the undergrowth.

I felt honoured to have seen such a thing.
A tiger.
Smiling.
A smiling tiger.

Such power,
Such beauty.

I turned,
Continued on my path.

Alone.

Ronan Flanagan (13)
Robert Gordon's College, Aberdeen

Tiger

Orange and black and yellow,
Eyes glowing,
Piercing the darkness,
Of the jungle.

Twigs snap,
Rustling of leaves,
Silent
And stealthily crouching
Near the helpless prey.

Waiting for the perfect moment,
He strikes, in a flash of black and orange,
Now everything comes to rest,
The triumphant tiger,
Waiting . . . just waiting.

David Young (13)
Robert Gordon's College, Aberdeen

Cat

Oh, what shall I do?
It's lying on my favourite mat!
It's waiting there so peacefully,
Oh, what shall I do?

I know!
I will take my favourite mat
And budge my favourite cat.
No!
It's waiting there so peacefully.

Oh, I wish it would just move,
But why is it not moving?

I know!
I will tempt, with the cat's favourite dish!
A bowl of fish!

That did not work!
What shall I do now?

I know!
I will scare it off;
I do not care about the cat,
I just want my favourite mat.

'Why!' I shout,
It is not moving,
I pick it up.
It is cold,
It gives me a chill.

I realise.

It is dead.
Oh no!

I have been so mean,
What have I done?
I have been so mean.

Oh, what shall I do?

Andy Davie (13)
Robert Gordon's College, Aberdeen

The Bear

In the Canadian mountainside
I was watching the view and walking,
Just walking,
When a giant blocked my path.
How majestic he looked.
In front of me, blocking my path.

'Please stand aside, oh noble creature,
Please let me be on my way,
Please let me go; I mean you no harm,
Please will you step out of my way?'

He growled at me.
The trespasser.
The threat.

This was his land.
I should not have been there.
There he ruled,
And there he stayed.

'Please stand aside, oh noble creature,
Please let me be on my way,
Please let me go; I mean you no harm,
Please will you step out of my way?'

He gambolled off with elegance,
Letting me pass through.
But now I feel regret,
I wished he'd stayed a moment longer,
He was better than the view.

Jack Abbott (13)
Robert Gordon's College, Aberdeen

Hunting Of Prey

As I stalked under the midnight sky,
Humming a harmonious tune to thee,
Upon my awakening, upon my encounter,
Stood a tall, dark creature shaded in the mist.

It was not cautious; it was abrupt,
It bowed its head with adequate grace,
I felt as if *I* were intruding in *its* space,
I stood there pondering questions,
Should I bow?
Should I run?
Should I stand still for just a few more minutes?
Oh, so very still.

Looking this mysterious creature in the eyes,
I raised my hand to touch skin to skin.
First it shunned, but then relaxed,
It stepped forward and . . .

Bang!

The shot of gunfire,
The animal's lank figure lay,
Blood oozing from its sleek, tender body,
All of its beauty, all of its grace and all of my faith,
Had changed to sadness and anger, in the matter of a second.

I wanted to hurt the person that had shot this innocent animal,
As the animal lay, tears welled up in my eyes.
I just did not want to accept the death of this pure, golden being,
Who could do such a crime
And yet not care that this being had had life?
That this murderer had grasped life and death with one hand,
I still ask myself these questions
And yet I still have no answers.

Katie Thompson (13)
Robert Gordon's College, Aberdeen

Stallion

A beast, so majestic,
A beast, so grand,
A beast, so beautiful,
An unknown entity.

The stallion,
Hooves as big as one man's fists,
Yet so much more powerful.
The stallion,
With a neigh identical to the one of a man's horse,
Yet so much more meaningful.

So dependant they are,
So dependant on each other,
So dependant on each other's guard,
So dependant on each other, that the other's life
Is of equal value as their own.

And why are they so dependant?
Because of our selfishness!
Because of our greed!
Because of us!

We have taken over,
We humans, us people, have taken them.
We have taken their brothers, their sisters
And we have used them.
Used them for a purpose of much less value
Than their jobs of protecting each other.

So why do we do this?
Why do we do this to a beast
So majestic?
To a beast, so grand?
To a beast, so beautiful?
I'll tell you why,
Because they are an unknown entity.

Hannah MacPherson (13)
Robert Gordon's College, Aberdeen

The Wolf

Cold, cold snow biting away at my face;
The Arctic desert stirring jerkily all around me,
So cold, how cold it is.

But wait! A sound, quietly in the distance,
I trudged on, not knowing what lay ahead,
In this treacherous, barren land.

I had stumbled into the land of deadly predators,
A sudden fear grew inside me, now aware I was being watched,
Something, silently, stalking.

As my sense of uneasiness grew,
I at once felt their presence,
Wolves, lots of wolves.

I was in their territory,
There was no use for running,
I was helpless.

And so they appeared,
Coming out of the blinding snow,
I was surrounded . . .

The pack moved in on me in perfect fashion,
Menacingly growling
And then it stopped.

A lone hunter came out from the trees and smelled me,
He lay down aside me
And made it a picturesque view: me and my friend.

Matthew Watt (13)
Robert Gordon's College, Aberdeen

Osprey

Gracefully flying in the winter's sky,
A grey and white osprey ascending high,
Glides down to meet,
The sparkling blue water.

As it takes off again, like a plane from a runway,
The wind passes through its feathery body.

Salmon slithering through the water,
Catches the eye of the osprey,
Its sharp, pointed face looks down.

Nosediving down low,
As fast as the wind can blow;
Claws appear out,
Followed by the scale-covered legs.

A splash appears from the fish in the water;
A final cry before it meets its predator's

Claws!

In the clutch of the osprey's claws,
The silvery slither wriggles in pain,
A fine feast for,
A flying hunter.

Sat up in the family nest,
Dealing out a piece of the catch,
Hungry mouths tweet,
For a bit of fish!

Peter Clark (13)
Robert Gordon's College, Aberdeen

A Wander

Wandering through the winter night,
Wondering at my awful plight.

A graceful bird,
Tonight my third,
Danced, carefree,
For me to see.

That bird,
My third,
My spirits raised.

That bird helped ease my awful plight,
My third that night.

I wished,
I fished,
As well as him,
To feed a family to the brim.

While wandering through the winter night,
Wondering at my awful plight.

Jennifer Sumner (14)
Robert Gordon's College, Aberdeen

Being Me

Why can't they accept me the way I really am?
Just because I don't dress the same,
Does that mean I need a nasty name?
Just because I don't wear a short skirt,
Does that mean they need to treat me like dirt?
Just because my hair's not poker-straight,
Does that mean I won't get a date?
If I don't change what I wear,
Will it always be this unfair?

Fidelma Beagan (14)
Rudolf Steiner School, Edinburgh

What If?

What if angry looks could kill?
Would we still exist
Or would we have murdered all our friends?

What if happy smiles could grant wishes?
Would we all be as rich as kings
Or as beautiful as the sun?

What if glares could penetrate walls?
Would we still have houses to live in?
What if fake smiles could deceive?
Would we all be liars?

What if tears could rend the heart?
Would we all be torn to shreds
Or have no hearts at all?

What if glowing faces could warn you?
Would all the winter clothes shops have closed down?
Would we all go around in swimsuits?

What if loving looks could protect us?
Would we all be shielded against everything
Or just have given up loving?
What if stares could dissolve us?
Would we all be puddles of slime?

What if scowls made the sky fall in?
Would we even have lasted a second
Let alone into the 21st century?
What if our faces stuck when the wind changed?
We would probably look very strange!

Tara Wight (14)
Rudolf Steiner School, Edinburgh

In Pursuit Of Happiness

He complains about his sister,
She complains about her mother,
They complain about their father
And all of them about their brother.
Sam complains about the weather,
Penelope is hating school,
Joe has had enough of work
And Tom's upset "Cause he's not cool!'
She's a typical teenager,
As her gran has pointed out,
She gets annoyed for being judged
And flounces off, her lips in a pout.
He got dumped and also sacked
And now is very fond of drink,
He's not only forgotten how to smile,
He's also forgotten how to think.
He is telling her it won't work
And they can't be together,
She is telling him it will work
And they'll be a couple forever!
She's had enough of doing it all,
But he can't even change a nappy,
In this turbulent world of troubles,
Can anyone truly say 'I'm happy'?

Helen Keller (14)
Rudolf Steiner School, Edinburgh

Our Secret Place

A little clearing, small,
Yet big, surrounded by plants, trees,
Flowers, the middle of nowhere, yet
The centre of everything. Hidden,
Completely hidden, hidden from the world.

The sky above, blue as the sea,
Scorching summer sun beats down,
Dappled by trees, dancing
On the water. The lake
Huge and still,
Untouched, untold
Occasional swan floats silently past,
Not a ripple, not a sound.

Hours and hours spent down here,
Days and days,
Promises made, secrets shared,
But not a word spoken.

One word could break the spell,
End the dream,
One word will lose this place
Forever.

This is our secret.

Kirsty Shinton (14)
Rudolf Steiner School, Edinburgh

What's Normal . . . Really?

Everyone is individual
So why do they try so hard to be the same?
If it's so easy to be strange
Shouldn't managing to be normal and ordinary be weird?
Who wants to be like everyone else?
You are who you are and there is nothing you can change
Not hiding behind a mask
No one can keep it up
Be yourself
There are so many personalities, but only one normal
It's normal to be weird!

Kavita Rittoo (13)
Rudolf Steiner School, Edinburgh

Fly Away

Sometimes I feel I want to get away,
break these chains, make my own way.
Go with the winds, like a blow-away kite,
soar like a bird and just take flight.
For all of life's troubles, to give it a rest,
would be just bliss, a weight off my chest.
Lighter and lighter and lighter I'd feel,
to be continuously rolling like a runaway wheel.
Now, this is it. To escape is my plan,
I can't go alone, come, take my hand.

Andrew Jones (15)
St Joseph's Academy, Kilmarnock

No Life At All

My life is black, my life is bleak,
I can't help that I can't speak.

My voice is so quiet, it's on the inside,
I'm in my own world, I feel so confined.

Do people laugh or do they stare?
I don't know, I can't see them there.

Am I different or am I the same?
What have I done? Who is to blame?

God? My parents? Didn't they try
To make me the same as my brothers, oh why . . .

Am I deaf and blind and I can't speak?
Some people must think I am a freak.

I am a triplet, one of three,
I wish you could feel what it's like to be *me!*

Megan Latta (13)
St Kentigern's RC Academy, Blackburn

Weather

S nowflakes glide down from the sky
N ight is perfect for snow to fly
O pportunities for snowball fights
W icked wind wrapped round me tight

R ampaging out in the wind
A gainst my window *bang, bang, bang*
I n my house is where I'll stay till it's over
N othing but puddles on the ground

S hining all round the town
U nder the shade is where I go
N o one wants to be inside.

Conor Galloway (13)
St Kentigern's RC Academy, Blackburn

Misunderstood Teenagers

Teenagers, teenagers, where do I start?
Misunderstood with their pieces of art,
On bus shelters, lamp posts and even on walls,
Some of it's smart, but some not at all.

Down the street on a Friday night,
Oh, what a very unpleasant sight,
Burberry scarf, Buckfast bottle and a fag in the hand,
Oh, what a way to waste this lovely land.

Not all teenagers are like that though,
It's such a shame that everyone thinks so,
Some just sit and do homework all night,
When they go down the street they get such a fright.

Friday nights bring drunken fights,
Buckfast bottles smacked off heads,
Teenagers end up in hospital beds,
How can we live in such a world?
Some teenagers are just not right in the head.

Will drunken teenagers ever keep friends?
They never seem to be sober,
So how do they know who are friends
And who are not?

At last, I leave you thinking,
Enjoy your youth, do stupid things,
We're only human after all,
But don't waste your time, spend it with friends
And all the laughs and fun will never end!

Amanda Love (13)
St Kentigern's RC Academy, Blackburn

A Watery Grave - The Sinking Of The Titanic

The smell of sea salt nipped the air,
Her hair fluttered in the breeze,
The sound of laughter could be heard,
As she gazed upon the seas.

A sudden crunch, a child's cry,
Panic rose all around,
Laughter was halted, the air grew cold,
As they listened for another sound.

Silent sobbing, trembling bodies,
The captain arrived on deck,
Bravely announced that something is wrong
And sent some people to check.

Men arrived back, their faces grey,
Tears rolling down their cheeks,
They tell of a crack and gushing water,
Caused by a giant ice peak.

The lifeboats were dropped into the sea,
Bobbing around on the waves,
Women and children were lowered down,
The men still hoped to be saved.

The smell of sea salt nipped the air,
Her hair clung to her neck,
The sound of sobbing could he heard,
As she gazed upon the wreck.

Down into the depths it did sink,
Silent as the grave,
She closed her eyes and said a prayer,
For the men they did not save.

Sorcha Rankine (13)
St Kentigern's RC Academy, Blackburn

Monsters

There's a monster in my bedroom!
There's a monster in my bed!
There's a gremlin in my closet!
And a spider on my head!

I don't know why they follow me,
Creep up on me and shout, *'Boo!'*
There's even a ghoul in my toilet,
When I'm going to the loo!

There's a mummy wrapped in bandages,
Who groans under the stairs,
There's a witch in the kitchen
And in the living room, some bears.

These monsters are so scary,
They make me cry and scream,
But then I wake up suddenly
And it was all a dream!

Liam McCombie (12)
St Kentigern's RC Academy, Blackburn

Football

If you're feeling down
And you are in a mood
Just play football
It's really, really good

Just grab a ball
And head to the park
But watch out for the dogs
They'll *bark, bark, bark*

Then find a pair of goals
And decide the teams
Play for a while
And see who's supreme.

Connor Riley (13)
St Kentigern's RC Academy, Blackburn

The Meaning Of Life

L ive to be loved
I n time you'll know
F or your timer will end
E veryone's will

I f you abuse yourself
S cars remain and that's you

E verything you do
T ime is still the king
E nding your timer is one
R esting in happiness is two
N ever waking from an eternal dream
A lways wondering and asking
L ooking for the meaning of life.

Joe Barron (12)
St Kentigern's RC Academy, Blackburn

The Shopping Centre

The shopping centre
Noisy and loud
Busy with frowns
When I go home, I'm out for the count.
I go there with all my mates
Or with boys on our dates.
Shopping is my favourite thing
When I'm wearing all my bling
I spend, spend, spend
Until the day comes to an end
The shopping centre is my best friend!

Nicola Sweeney (13)
St Kentigern's RC Academy, Blackburn

Time

There's a clock on the wall
That's neither big, nor small
It ticks, it tocks
Like so many other clocks.

But there was something different
About this certain clock
Not the cogs nor the hands
Nor the pattern, white as chalk.

But, the man called Time
Who lived behind the face
He disappeared one dark night
And left without a trace.

Now, the clock soon stopped, to the owner's despair
So he sent for Time
But Time didn't come to see the clock
But he sent a little sign.

It said:
Dear owner of the precious clock
I can't come to help right now
I'm helping out the world's clocks
Which are rough like an old man's frown
The hands have stopped, the faces chipped
And the pendulums are stuck.
The paint is faded, the cogs are jammed
And the clocks are dented and stuck
So dear owner, I will be back soon
To repair your clock
If it's stuck or if it's stopped
I'll make it go *tick-tock, tick-tock.*

Matthew McCafferty (12)
St Kentigern's RC Academy, Blackburn

Weather Noises

A lightning flash
A rumble in the sky
A shower of rain
Comes from the night sky
A howl from the wind
A thud from the rain
A dripping sound
Coming from the outside drain.

Lauren McCairn (12)
St Kentigern's RC Academy, Blackburn

Rain

Drip, drop, drip, drop

The rain comes pouring down
The clouds are crying
Night and day

Drip, drop, drip, drop

The rain is always dripping
The rain is always dropping

Drip, drop, drip, drop!

Sarah Cook (12)
St Kentigern's RC Academy, Blackburn

The Sky

I love the sky,
With birds flying high,
White, fluffy clouds passing by.
At night, with the moon shining brightly,
The stars twinkling ever so slightly,
I love the sky.

Sean Steedman (12)
St Kentigern's RC Academy, Blackburn

Bullying

B ullies are bad
U nkind and sad
L ying and cheating
L ike a good beating
Y et why be a bully?

Jennifer Bett (12)
St Kentigern's RC Academy, Blackburn

Life

L ive, understand and enjoy your life
I n fun, priceless mischief
F lood your mind with exciting memories
E xplore life as if you're high up in the trees!

Mark Hamill (12)
St Kentigern's RC Academy, Blackburn

Life

L ive life to the very max
I gnore people that try to make it sad
F ulfil every goal and dream
E verybody has the chance to use it!

Alanah Rodgers (12)
St Kentigern's RC Academy, Blackburn

Sad Moments

T ick-tock
I nteresting lives
M y papa died
E veryone is so sad.

Jhordan Tease (12)
St Kentigern's RC Academy, Blackburn

Life

L ive your life to the full
I t's too short to be boring
F ulfil your dreams and
E verything will be OK!

Ross Wilkinson (12)
St Kentigern's RC Academy, Blackburn

Life

L ife is precious
I t's long or short
F antastic or miserable
E veryone lives, everyone dies.

Mark McNulty (12)
St Kentigern's RC Academy, Blackburn

Time

T ime
I s of the essence
M emories are precious
E njoy them while you can.

Ellie Fordyce (12)
St Kentigern's RC Academy, Blackburn

Time

T ime is precious
I t should be cherished
M ake it count
E njoy it.

Nicole McGarty (12)
St Kentigern's RC Academy, Blackburn

The Life Of A Musician

The nerves are racked up ten storeys high,
You're going out there to touch the sky.
You're only thinking about how you can ruin
And you're sweating as if it's the month of June.

                    The audience is out there, ready to load,
                    They're waiting for you to come out and explode,
                    You can hear them chanting and clapping their hands,
                    But you need them as they're your most loyal fans.

You walk to the stage, you're going to collapse,
But you pick yourself up, your guitar in your grasp,
You strum the first chord and see everyone there,
You stop for a sec and breathe in the fresh air.

                    You're starting to play now and singing as well,
                    After all, you've got music to sell,
                    The crowd just love you when you've got that guitar
                    And you've got that feeling; I'm gonna go so far.

The show's finishing now and just as well,
You want to go home and lie down for a spell,
You're up early tomorrow so you'll be tired too . . .
But you're a musician and that's what you do!

Philip McLean (13)
St Kentigern's RC Academy, Blackburn

Life

L ife is precious, cherish it while you can
I mpossible is nothing, just be a man
F alling over is a part of life, but you can still get up
E veryone is different, some say 'Hello!', some say 'Hi!'
   And some people just say ''S'up!'

Christie McKenna (12)
St Kentigern's RC Academy, Blackburn

Being Famous

I have to be
A role model,
Being snapped
By paparazzi
Isn't such a doddle.

I attend award
Ceremonies
And premieres
Galore.

When I go
To the corner store,
They're watching
Me.

I wish they would
Just let me be,
Rumours leak
Until my temper
Reaches its peak.

I'm always in the papers
When I don't look my best,
They always pick the pictures
I really do detest!

Although I feel honoured
To be admired,
Being followed around all day
Makes me very tired.

Hannah O'Donnell (13)
St Kentigern's RC Academy, Blackburn

Life

L ife is precious
I t is time well spent
F ind the fun in it
E veryone does

I t is a special time for us to enjoy
S avour it when you can

P eople love, people hate, make the most of what you get
R ight or left, you are no different
E ach person, good or bad, deserves a chance
C all your mum, call your dad and tell them you're not sad
I ntelligence means nothing when it comes down to life
O utside people starve, but they make the most of it
U gly or nice, make the most of your life
S o keep your loved ones close.

Ryan Hamill (12)
St Kentigern's RC Academy, Blackburn

Stop Bullying

Groups of friends having fun,
All day long in the sun.
Wouldn't you like to be one of them?
Stop bullying and start again.

I don't know who or what you are,
But I can see you're bullying from afar.
Stop blaming people for things that are on your mind,
Stop bullying and being unkind.

Laura Weir (12)
St Kentigern's RC Academy, Blackburn

Love

Love is like a bird in the sun,
You can see the beauty or turn and run,
Run away to paradise where life flows like a river,
No trouble, no sign of an ending.

If you look into the deep pools,
In that special one's eyes,
You can read your happy future like a classical book.
Just take a moment, a moment in time,
To gaze and have a proper look.

You can see two wrinkled hands,
Together, never to separate,
The beauty of love lasts forever for them,
Until the end of their story.

Each time the three-word sentence is said,
It grows deep into the other lover.
Listened to, thought over, one thousand times.
If those three words fell into the ocean,
They would not lose their meaning
Until that sentence was found.

A child's hand crawls silently, to link to another,
Beginners in the mystery of love.
There is no dark, forgotten corner in this world,
Where the magic can be forgot.

Flora Ogilvy (12)
St Leonards School, St Andrews

The Child Refugee

Cold, scared and misunderstood,
I'm a child refugee.
I've had to abandon my own family,
To escape a terrible fate.

Murder and death is everywhere,
War has broken out.
Nowhere to go,
Nowhere to hide.

Marked down as a refugee,
Unwanted by everyone.
No one wants to know,
No one cares.

All I want is help,
Some care and some compassion.
And I am sure,
That the tables will soon turn.

So far, no help has come,
No hand to hold or shoulder to cry on.
But I'm sure help will come soon,
It has to . . .

Callum Robertson (12)
St Leonards School, St Andrews

The Drunk Driver

I didn't see it coming
I didn't even know
All I was doing was humming
I had a sort of glow

My mother had told me that morning
'Look before you cross'
I did and there was no warning
So I began to walk across

As I walked I began thinking
What was mother so afraid of?
He must think he's a king
And must not believe in love

I felt it as he hit me
And then everything went black
I wonder if he felt glee
As he drove, never looking back?

Mother says he was a 'drunk driver'
A man who doesn't feel
I'm lucky, I was a survivor
From an attack of a drunk in an automobile.

Philippa Kyle (12)
St Leonards School, St Andrews

Waiting

I am waiting,
Just waiting
For someone to come and
Take me away from this place.

I don't know how long
I have been here for,
I don't even know
Why I'm here.

I have so many questions,
Why am I here?
Who are my parents?
What was wrong with me?

People don't tell me anything
About my past.
I just have to guess,
And imagine.

I just wish I knew who they were!
If I have any other relations!
Why don't they look after me?
Why do I have to stay here?

I want to live in a nice house,
With people who love me
And care for me.
Is that too much to ask?

Henrietta Barton (12)
St Leonards School, St Andrews

Thoughts

Words can mean a lot
But sometimes they don't
All I wanted was the truth
That's something I wish I'd known

Hold me in your arms
Kiss me in the rain
You said you'd always love me
That love can turn to pain

I wish you wouldn't talk to me
I wish you would go away
Always with your lame remarks
Every single day

Your words used to hurt me
You think you're all 'that'
All you seem to me now
Is some self-obsessed brat

I still think about you
But I have moved on
Still every single thought
Makes me want to yawn

Say what you want to say
You're just wasting your time
This is my life, and what it used to be
In a little rhyme.

Dana Beaton (12)
St Leonards School, St Andrews

Crystal Dreams

A twirling sparkle gleaming in the icy light
Glassy talons encircle one and all
A soft white layer falls on the ground
Everyone beneath not making a sound

They twist and dance until they lay
Each one different from the rest
Dazzling patterns stunning to the eye
As they tumble they seem to fly

So much pleasure to be had
Excitement shared by everyone
Children ecstatic to see the sight
Anticipating a day of delight

Shining angels across the land
Each with a unique memory attached
Crystal wings shining bright
All imprinted in the white

But all too soon they fade away
Turning the Earth green once more
All their witnesses besotted
This time will never be forgotten.

Charlotte Zajicek (15)
St Leonards School, St Andrews

Pain Inside

She's said that day was the worse,
It was such a cliché,
She'd said she'd needed my help,
But I pushed her away.

I ignored her cries of pain,
As she nursed her own bruises,
I was too involved with myself,
This way everyone loses.

The next day she was gone,
She hadn't left a letter,
They said she died in her sleep,
But I thought I knew better . . .

I searched day and night,
For that one tiny clue,
Then I realised myself,
It was physical abuse.

There are so many out there,
That no one can save,
They take their secret with them,
Right to the grave . . .

Lily Watts (12)
St Leonards School, St Andrews

Somaliland, You Are My Hope

Time was over for the ill and rotten union that formed Somalia,
In 1992 the terrible dictator who ruled Somalia was overthrown,
His last order was to bomb Hargeisa,
Capital of independent Somaliland,
Which at that time was the last bastion of Somali liberty.

For moments the American-sponsored bombs flouted the sky,
And then they hit the town and destroyed every house,
Children were torn apart but even that could not save the
                                   bloodthirsty dictator,
Out of the ashes of Hargeisa rose, like a falcon, a new state,
It was to be the greatest and strongest the world was ever to see.

The new state was called Somaliland,
It stayed firm and resisted American invasion.
Somalia contracted the illness of anarchy,
The inhabitants of Mogadishu were sliced into pieces,
Cut up between the bayonets of the soldiers in the battle
                                   for Mogadishu.

During the time of genocide,
In which the Shabelle river was coloured red by blood,
The Somalilandish people didn't join in the sanguinary killings,
Which took place in Mogadishu,
They didn't give in to the temptation to rob and kill their
                                   own neighbours.

The Somalilandish people held together,
And rewrote their future,
They chased to Hell their suppressors,
And created democracy, not anarchy and suppression,
With a will of iron, they overcame the extraordinary obstacles
                                   in their way.

Somaliland,
Land of flowers,
Land of freedom,
Land of democracy,
You are my hope.

Colin Cortbus (12)
St Leonards School, St Andrews

The Rose

My heart fills with warmth as I look at you,
You remind me of the sweet scent of spring,
The tender touch of summer,
But most of all beauty!

You look as though you were kissed by angels
And individually carved in God's hands,
Your colour fills the world with lustre
And puts smiles on everyone's faces.

Every tiny part of you represents pure love,
You are wholesome and unspoiled,
You are gentle and selfless,
You make every day brighter.

You can mend a broken heart,
You can fill a dream with delight and riches,
You can make someone feel complete,
But when you are given as a present, you can make someone
feel loved!

Anais De Villiers (13)
St Leonards School, St Andrews

Global Warming

We watched in silence as the ice crashed down
Breathtaking to watch, yet frightening to see
Ice floes now stretch where polar bears once played
Time has run out, but are we to blame?

The signs had been there for all to see
From the might of Katrina to the hole in our sky
But we looked elsewhere while the damage was done
We are to blame, but has time run out?

The future looks different, uncertain and dark
Our planet is shifting and changing too fast
Perhaps there's a window before all is lost
No time for blame, our future is at stake.

Lauren Sandeman (13)
St Leonards School, St Andrews

The Heart Attack

Turning back time
I wish it could be done
But I didn't know it would happen
I thought the holiday would be fun

We got on the plane
Everything was fine
He looked like he was happy
He even had some wine

Then he complained
A pain in his chest
He started to gasp
And everyone was stressed

My dad survived
He feels no more pain
And all I say now is
I hope it doesn't happen again.

Claire Ford (12)
St Leonards School, St Andrews

Flying

If I could fly
I'd fly all over the world
I'd fly to Paris
I'd fly to New York

I would fly to the plumbing shop in Brazil
I would fly to the football with my Uncle Phil
Stockport 3, Leyton Orient 0
Then I must fly home until tomorrow night.

Ged Rutherford (12)
St Leonards School, St Andrews

It's All Over Now

(In memory of my brother Dougal, who died from cancer, aged 6)

He lies there,
Just like he did yesterday,
Strapped down to a bed, with no colour.
He can see them,
So can I;
The white coats and masks.
They're everywhere.
I can hear him screaming,
The beeping of the machines,
The pumping of gas.
It's all new to him.
He has wires, going in, going out.
He's scared,
So am I.
I can't just stand here
And let them do this to him.
He's crying,
He hates it.
They stick needles and wires into him.
He screams.
It's all over.
Another day passes.
I'm all alone.
I love him,
I miss him.
It's all over now.

Cecilia Stewart-Wilson (12)
St Leonards School, St Andrews

Teddy, Teddy

Teddy, teddy
You're so sweet
Teddy, teddy
With missing feet
Teddy, teddy
I love you so
Teddy, teddy
You'll never be a foe
Teddy, teddy
With a matted coat
Teddy, teddy
In a makeshift boat
Teddy, teddy
How I should have saved you
Teddy, teddy
Instead of tying my shoe
Teddy, teddy
I'll never forget when you drowned
Teddy, teddy
I'll not rest until you are found.

Laurie Johnston (12)
St Leonards School, St Andrews

The Statue

The middle of the sea,
That's where I am,
Where the waves are white, angry horses,
They don't stop, they don't tire,
The wind flies like an albatross,
Carrying cold, misery and death,
But I stay still.

Adam Harris (13)
St Leonards School, St Andrews

What Am I?

I am wilder than the wildest beast,
I am loud and boisterous,
I am wild in light and dark,
What am I?

I am cruel and full of spite,
I am ugly and unfair,
I am cruel in country and town,
What am I?

I am more beautiful than a clear sunset,
I am pure and joyful,
I am beautiful over hill and dale
What am I?

I puzzle even the greatest brains,
I even drive people mad,
For you see they cannot find the point of me -
I am life!

Susie Cronin (13)
St Leonards School, St Andrews

Eagle Eyes

The eagle high in the sky,
Perched on the unclimbable cliff,
Searching the deep, deep sea.

Razor-sharp talons ready to grasp its prey,
Unweary eyes ready for any movement,
Swooping down fast and mercilessly,
Just out of reach, but not for long.

Steven Farrell (12)
St Leonards School, St Andrews

Imagine

Here I am,
Alone,
Sitting on a bench,

And then it comes,
The imagination,
A wonder.

First you go through a time hole,
Up the stair from there to there,
Then you bob around there for a bit,
Then all of a sudden,
Anything you want can become real.
At first I imagine a forest,
With lots of animals and trees,
A man comes at me with a knife,
So I decide to go somewhere else.
Then I go to somewhere cold, hard and mean,
A wooden building leans over,

For of course the demon of man
Has a grasp which pierces the skin of kindness,
So I go into the house
And then there is the most beautiful creature.
But then the deception,
I know because it is me, who imagines,
It takes off its beautiful mask and screeches with bloodlust,
Then I spin and swirl,

My train arrives for school.

Marcus Bodzioch (12)
St Leonards School, St Andrews

How To Be Dead . . .

A tainted vision scratched in my mind,
A darkened secret locked up inside,
A ghostly nothingness where love should hang,
A profound hurt cuts deep.

Thrown out by God, abandoned by hope,
Existence means nothing, how can I cope?
Forgotten by family, abused with lie on top of lie,
I break down at night howling, my cheeks stained with tears as I cry.

Put down by love, blown out by light,
Should I give up, disappear into the night?
Illtreated with trust, nothing to care for,
I sway back and forth, trembling with lunacy to the core.

Filled with hatred, speared by guilt,
My soul hastens to let go, as I slowly wilt.
Forged by the hand of egotism, veined with spite,
Should I end this wrong and do the thing that's right?

How I'm lost in a maze of fears so cold,
My mangled life sudden to lose hold,
How my heart beats no more,
Riddled with violence, crazed like war.

A tainted vision scratched in my mind,
A darkened secret locked up inside,
A ghostly nothingness where love should hang,
A profound hurt cuts deep.

Liam Deboys (14)
St Leonards School, St Andrews

Be Yourself

Everyone has a dream,
Some stronger than others,
They might have been seen,
Or discovered beside us

Sometimes you feel you're not yourself,
Or possibly trying to be someone else,
Popular or geeky,
Nerdy or freaky,
We are all different

Each and every one of us,
Has our own ability,
We don't need to make a fuss,
Because we have it anyway

We should have something to follow,
And set a goal,
Go for it all
And just let go

No person should ever give up,
All work hard,
And step the jump,
Spot the chance and take it,
Be yourself, don't fake it

If we want something enough,
Don't complain or take a fit,
Be tough,
And fight for it

We will only get far,
If we make our own decisions,
Do your best
And don't let anyone tell you who you are

Take any opportunity
And be who you want to be,
Don't worry,
Just be happy.

Emma Lindsay (13)
St Leonards School, St Andrews

Lost At Sea

Millennium night,
The last glowing embers of a thousand years,
Hover like shards of molten glass
And tumble erratically into the cool, silent water
Where I stand and contemplate
Celebration

Partying revellers call,
A hollow echo across the Tay
And the sky alight with glowing colours,
That reflect upon my own solemn face.

An exotic kaleidoscope forms across the sky,
To mark the end or the beginning?
My heart drums against my ribcage,
Like a desperate prisoner,
As I wade in.

The water of the Tay swirls at my feet,
Leaving its decay lying on the shore.
The icy reeds begin to creep around my feet, luring me in,
As the smooth, slippery rocks brush by.

I stand now, almost submerged,
Faltering slightly,
Like a flickering candle in the last nanosecond,
Before extinction.

My last glance at the colours,
And parties across the world,
Yet, I don't want this,
This life is not for me.

Michael Overend (13)
St Leonards School, St Andrews

Me And My Balloon

It is still and quiet
Not a sound to be heard
Just me and my balloon

No talking or chatter
No screeching or screaming
Just me and my balloon

The great blanket of blue
So high up above
Begins to cloud over
Like a handing-covering glove

The tip-tap of the rain
Increases very quick
As I hurry under a tree
My watch begins to tick

Tick-tock-tick
As the wind picks up
My hand is opened
And my balloon flies up

Twisting and turning
Soaring and swirling
I watch my balloon
Fly higher and higher

It is no longer visible
My head drops down
Nothing interesting now
Just me and the ground

It is still and quiet
Not a sound to be heard
Just me and no balloon.

Annabel Zajicek (12)
St Leonards School, St Andrews

Hoodie On A Street Corner

'A hoodie on a street corner',
Was out of school when he hit sixteen,
All his reports labelled him 'non-performer',
Thick, stupid; shouldn't be seen,
He's got no job, spends all day with his mates,
Everyone calls him a 'ned',
The person everyone loves to hate,
He thinks he should've just stayed in bed,
He doesn't know what to do,
The hoodie has feelings too.

'A hoodie on a street corner',
Does he drink Buckfast all night?
That's what's expected of him,
Out with his mates who all look a sight.
That's his place in society,
A thug, they say he has no propriety,
He doesn't know what to do,
The hoodie has feelings too.

'A hoodie on a street corner',
Sees an old woman trying to cross, he takes her arm,
Guides her safely through the congested cars and vans,
Causes her no alarm.
The hoodie carries her bags full of pots and pans,
They reach the other side,
He was the only one who tried,
He was the 'Good Samaritan', the one who succeeded,
To help when the woman needed.
The old woman didn't know what to do,
She realised the hoodie had feelings too.

Sarah Leith (15)
St Leonards School, St Andrews

The No Name Poem

The winds howled, the rain was horizontal,
The lone man walked at a fastened pace.
Faster and faster, then he stopped,
His silhouette outlined by the street lamps.
Why did he stop?
The thunder rumbled and crashed,
Lightning illuminated the land around.
How he trembled and quivered,
Like a mouse cornered by a car.
Where will he go? What will he do?
Suddenly, the rumbling stopped,
The wind was quiet,
The darkness faded away.
He stopped shivering and stood up,
The rain cleared and his brisk walk could continue,
Weaving around the puddles, continuing on his way.

Amy Clark (14)
St Leonards School, St Andrews

Remember

Down to Flanders Field
To the river of Somme,
To dead men's field
To the dead of Tom.

Fields of the poppy,
Mark the great blunder,
Where death was hobby
And air was thunder.

Dead lists were so tall,
By us remembered,
The many fallen,
In mid November.

Jamie Mansbridge (15)
St Leonards School, St Andrews

True Agony

I stood there with my gun in hand
I walked onto broken land
And over there, standing still
Was the man I longed to kill

The air was silent, the atmosphere tense
I had to remember this would all make sense
I slowly put my hand on the gun
I had to shoot him, I couldn't run

I moved my hand towards the trigger
Every second my fear grew bigger
I tried to shoot, but I suddenly stopped
That dreaded gun I slowly dropped

I picked up my gun off the dusty floor
I couldn't drop it, not once more
I took up my aim, for him it was the end
My finger on the trigger started to bend

I took the shot, the end was here
The bullet came out alongside a tear
The life I had ended, how selfish I was
I killed a man for one stupid cause

Fear turned to pain, pain to despair
I looked at the man lying dead over there
My hatred of myself grew bigger and bigger
And I had no hesitation on pulling the trigger.

Nick Shannon (13)
St Leonards School, St Andrews

The Tramp

I walk along the streets at night,
Glaring into the glistening moonlight.

People stop and stare at me,
Not with care, but with a glare.

I come across a penny on the street,
And think to myself, *oh, what a treat!*

For me, I have no more than this,
My coat, my hat and hopefulness.

I wish one day I could sail away to a land
Where I never have to pay for food or clothes or a home,
Who knows?

Well, here comes the morning, the sun is dawning.

For I am a tramp bent down by a post of a lamp,
Begging for money like a bear for his honey.

Charlotte Carswell (13)
St Leonards School, St Andrews

Lights

Lights are bright
Lights are dim
They can be just about everything
It lights up the sky as the sun
So we can see to have fun.

We don't like the dark
Because it is usually boring
But the light of the moon
Sets everything glowing.

Lights are everywhere for us to see
Lights help people, you and me!
Lights are there to help us through our troubles
But bright lights can sometimes give us the wobbles.

But lights are there to be very useful
And they are always very beautiful.

Bethan Owen (14)
St Leonards School, St Andrews

Second On The Right And Straight On 'Til Morning

To arrive at Peter Pan's place of dawning
Take the second on the right and straight on 'til morning.
Float with the sun and shoot with the stars,
Glide with the sun and slip by Mars.
Sail through galaxies and dance past probes,
Skate in circles around the globes.
Tumble and turn and splash and surge,
Swim through black holes and emerge.
Flutter and flap and drift and dive,
Touch ultimate limits and return alive.
Waft and wade and swirl and zoom,
Explode past planets with a boom.
Spiral and swish and swim and sway,
Flash past planets with colours gay.
Dashing and dawdling, singing and screaming,
Bobbing and bursting, drifting and dreaming.
And as the sun breaks the first rays of dawning,
Arrive at second on the right and straight on 'til morning.

Rebecca Mansbridge (13)
St Leonards School, St Andrews

St Andrews Beach

I rest and gaze at the waves rising high,
The colours incredibly shimmer in the sky,
They are all assorted shades of blue,
It makes such a breathtaking view.

The crash of waves along the beach,
Makes me want to distend and reach,
As the gulls screech in the sky,
The noise of jets startles them and they proceed by.

The grains of sand subside through my fingers
And the warm sun above lingers,
As the cool ice cream touches my lips,
The sand gets blown in my eyes and slowly nips.

The smell of seaweed in the air,
Grasps me as I eat a malleable, tasty pear
And the scent of the salty sea,
Tickles my nose and follows me.

Megan Lambert (14)
St Leonards School, St Andrews

Cat

Molly sat in my cot and kept me safe
When I was very small,
Staying patiently when I cried,
She didn't complain at all.

When Mummy was teaching me how to walk,
Molly always came too
And when I was ill, Molly was there,
Whether I had aches, pains or flu.

I loved Molly with all my heart,
From her claws to the tip of her fur.
We truly were the best of friends
And I never wanted to leave her.

Then one day I came home from school,
'We have some bad news,' my mum said
And I couldn't believe what I was hearing -
My dear Molly was dead.

Sophie Cole (14)
St Leonards School, St Andrews

The Caribbean

I sit here in the bitter wind,
Trying to imagine,
How awfully nice it would be,
In the Caribbean.

I dream on and on,
Wondering what is going on,
How many people are on the beach,
Ahh, life there would be as good as a peach.

Lots of people surfing the waves,
Maybe even some exploring caves.
The swaying trees and the rustling of leaves,
Being blown by the warm, warm breeze.

But as I sit here,
I must remember,
Even though I don't want to, I must,
The fact that it is all just a dream.

Fiona Baird (12)
St Leonards School, St Andrews

The Beggar

I sit on the streets every day, every night,
Thinking of what it would be like
To live in a house and have a family that cared,
Having a sibling who loved and shared.

But I can only watch the crowds walk by,
They do not care about me, I can see it in each of their eyes,
One by one they give me a glare,
It is as if they cannot help but stare.

I do tell myself it is all a dream,
But every time I pinch my skin, I just want to scream,
Because I do know that it is all true,
Whilst I sit here in this lonely avenue.

Every day I wait for someone to drop a penny,
To feed my little dog Lenny.
He has suffered days on end,
But he will always be my best friend.

I want to forget my past and look to my future,
As I hope it will not be as much torture.
But now I know and can see,
That I am a beggar and always will be.

Morven McCulloch (12)
St Leonards School, St Andrews

Morning, Noon And Night

It enters the sky,
Like a smiling face.
All lights up around.
The birds sing,
The birches blow
And flowers rise with welcoming arms,
Silently from the ground.

It keeps on rising,
Up through the scented air,
Like a giant hot air balloon.
A cool and refreshing breeze
Sends the clouds floating through
The bright and busy sky,
As beautiful as the starlit moon.

Evening comes,
All calms down.
The cheerful birds and breezes go.
Families retire from the tiresome day,
Busy workers are homeward bound
And the lights are put on and fires lit,
To carry on the warming glow.

Claudia Beasley (13)
St Leonards School, St Andrews

Gone

She lay there,
Hospital machines beeped constantly.
They said that she would be alright,
But I didn't believe them.
I tried to believe, but it's hard to
When you're so scared.
I sat there for hours,
Just watching her. Listening also,
Listening to her soft breath.
The room was grey, as was my mood.
My face was red and tear-stained,
But I didn't care.
A nurse came in to check on her,
She smiled at me sweetly.
I tried hard to smile back at her,
But I could only just manage to turn up
The corners of my mouth.
The nurse left again
And the corners of my mouth
Dropped back into place.
Suddenly, the beeping picked up its pace.
Her eyes flickered. She was trying to breathe.
Then suddenly, all was silent.
She was gone.

Olivia Cassidy (12)
St Leonards School, St Andrews

Lost For Words

My heart is thumping
Blood is running down my body
Hate stirs me
Like the whole world is full of hatred
As I try to get up
Force pushes me down
For I am just lying here
Lying in my pool of blood
No one is coming
I feel alone
Lying in the middle of nowhere
Lying in a field
I can hear a train coming a few yards down
I can taste blood
I feel so tired
My body feels broken
Like a broken saber

But I won't cry
I never cry
Even if I am half alive

I see spots now
Lots and lots of spots
Then a burst of light

Then I can see no more.

Emilie Chalmers (13)
St Leonards School, St Andrews

Starlight

Bitter cold swooped down
With darkness on its back.
My mood matched its misery
For warmth there was a lack.
Tonight no moon dare show its face
For fear of pleasing human race,
For now the day has bowed unto the starlight.

In this dim but beauteous glow,
A fantasy none dared to know,
A mystery lying in wait for those
Who can brave the darknesses coming.

For the stars will let your mind run free,
Transport you to another galaxy,
But where'er you go in sun or snow,
The stars will come there with you.

But now the cold and darkness come,
Unwelcomed by most, embraced by some,
For there are those who delight in the cover of dark,
But most share not this unsound view,
For those who welcome cover are the lying few,
For who could lie in the trusting exposure of starlight?

But dark, like evil, is overcome,
Like in a fantasy,
Against dark the stars have won.
One reign is now over,
A new ruler takes the throne,
For darkness was usurped by starlight.

Catriona Stirling (13)
St Leonards School, St Andrews

The Hitman's Life

My targets have numbers, one, two and three,
Killing them is a job to me,
For I am a hitman and I give it my all,
I have to see them tense then fall.

I feel no fear, sadness or joy,
I can only remember when I was a boy,
That my ambition was clear-cut and through,
My client now tells me where to find you.

I picture you in the crosshairs of my sight,
Just you and I on this cold, dark night,
That I, a hitman, that will end your life,
It could be the gun or even the knife.

The trigger, so cold and wonderfully smooth,
I'm waiting for you to make a final move.
That perfect shot, I have to pull
And then your eyes glaze and go dull.

The time has come, the moment is here,
That bullet comes speeding towards your ear.
The metal hits you clean in the head,
It's quiet and dark, now you are dead . . .

Joseph Levett (14)
St Leonards School, St Andrews

The Final Battle

I stood there in the gaping space,
Solemn emotion upon my face.
All around me, the gunshots fired,
I willed to be with the ones I admired.

One by one they all went down,
Endless gunfire, the only sound.
I watched my friends and comrades fall,
I mourned the terrible death of them all.

But as a soldier I had to go on,
Motivated by our army songs.
I looked towards the deserted sky,
Thinking that surely I must die.

I ducked down low, and out of sight,
Moving on with my greatest might.
I stood up tall, and I was hit,
Falling to the ground, my eyes no longer lit.

I lay down now, in all my pain,
Grasping on to my name tag chain.
That was it, I was gone,
The battle seemed so ever long.

My soul deserted to the sky,
On the ground, cold I lie.
But up in Heaven my soul will rest,
With the ones, that I love best.

Iain Watson (13)
St Leonards School, St Andrews

The Passionate Aviator

The sun danced on the water as my craft's shadow fell over me.
Slowly opening the door
Was like opening a new world that I owned and had to control.
I sat in the cockpit staring at the controls and gauges . . .
I knew all too well, for I had familiarised myself with them
Over the last few weeks.
I inserted the key and turned it slowly,
Holding the throttle firmly.
The engine roared to life
And immediately I could feel the power at my fingertips.
My mind and heart were racing, going over the pre-flight checks.
I fastened my harness, for this would be the ride of a lifetime.
I released the brakes with my feet,
For that was the last thing holding me back from my dream.
Easing the power in made the engine grow louder,
Thousands of butterflies filled my body as I began to move.
I lost myself for one second
In the presence of such excitement and fear,
Quickly gaining control.
I steered my craft towards and onto the taxi-way.
I sat paused in my plane
Staring down the long, beautiful runway.
Smiling to myself,
I opened the throttle and accelerated into adulthood.

Adriaan de Villiers (15)
St Leonards School, St Andrews

Disco Inferno

One, two, three, four,
The rhythmic beat of the bass
Pulsates through the room,
With each set of four livelier than the last.
Feet begin to tap,
Lights start to flash,
The volume pumps to the point
That all that is left is the tune,
Electrifying the atmosphere
And surging through the people.
The floor bounces with a timely burst of feet,
Hammering down and springing up,
Whilst heads and arms
Are carelessly thrown in all directions.
The blaring music, the blinding lights
And beating feet, all build up to a blistering bang!
Sparks fly, fire strikes.
Disco inferno.

Kenneth Reid (14)
St Leonards School, St Andrews

Good Times, Great Memories

Waiting for the taxi, *peep, peep!*
Excited to get on the train.
Meeting a taxi for the caravan park.
Yes, hurrah! We've arrived.
Seeing the arcade and the club.
Buying sweets and Coke in the shop.
Another time at the beach.
Yes, yes, yes!

Christopher Ricketts (14)
St Ninian's High School, Glasgow

Bully

I was standing in the middle of the playground,
By myself.
I could see the bully coming,
I couldn't move, I was so petrified,
Even though I felt like running.

The bully is bigger than me,
He is as big as a pig,
As tall as a tree.

Then he came and pushed me to my knees,
Picked me up and punched me in the face.
When he left, I was shaking like a leaf,
I felt like a disgrace.

Then next thing I knew, I was in maths,
The bully made a joke and everyone laughs.
I felt so sad that I wanted to cry,
I knew I shouldn't, the bully wouldn't.

Before I knew it, it was lunch,
Again in the playground by myself.
I could see the bully coming,
He came over and pushed me to my knees again.
When he pulled me up,
Instead of punching me,
I pushed him in the muck.

David McNeilage (13)
St Ninian's High School, Glasgow

Garelochead

G eorge walking in the sun almost as if he had the best fun

A bseiling from boulders 10ft high, just like falling from the sky

R apid rivers gave me the shivers

E veryone shaking, saying they can't do it, but I was the one saying
I can canoe it!

L ove was in the air with a boy I met there

O h, joyful memories from that place where I won the silly race!

C an we stay another week, because we still need to play
hide-and-seek?

H iding in the hot summer sun, I was having amazing fun

E very day was a new adventure, singing songs and jogging along

A lways remember great memories there, never forget the smell of
the air

D ogs were barking, it was fun. Always remember the fun in the sun!

Kerry Shields (14)
St Ninian's High School, Glasgow

My Grandpa's War Memories

It was too quiet, you could hear the roar of the sea,
You could hear clicking as the ammunition was almost set free.
Standing in the landing craft I was scared,
I came to hear that the enemy was there.
The whistle went, the landing craft door slammed,
The enemy started shooting like charging bulls.
I used my head to cover the debris as it was not friendly.
My brothers fell, but I was well.
I felt a pain, I was to blame.
I fell into mire, I escaped for a while,
As I was almost in the pile.
I was wounded, the enemy treated me nice,
But I was so sorry for those that lost their lives.
I must fight, fight, fight!

Connor Hughes (12)
St Ninian's High School, Glasgow

Away With Words

I looked down at the others
As I sat up here alone,
Surrounded by my enemies, she sat down on her throne.

She looked at me and sighed
And to her friends I knew she'd lied.

She stood up and walked towards me,
A fearsome bully, that's all I could see.

To her this torture seemed like fun
But to me it was like a bullet being shot from a gun.

The sweat dripped from her head,
Her bullying me made me wish I was dead.
Then suddenly she said to me, 'Give me your lunch,
I need something to munch.'

If only she could see,
What it's like to be me.

Jade Jarvie (12)
St Ninian's High School, Glasgow

I Am Rich

I am as rich as a queen bee,
With swarms of money buzzing around me.
Playing music here, playing music there, playing music everywhere.
Everyone shouting my name, Michael, Michael!
Like lots of monkeys screaming night and day.

I would like it all to stop right now,
Mopping sweat from my brow.
I wonder what it would be like to be one of them,
Running about.
Would I like it, would I not?
I could try it, or should I not?
I am as rich as a queen bee,
With lots of money buzzing around me.

Michael Finlayson (12)
St Ninian's High School, Glasgow

Turning Back Time

Right, now I had a really hard test
Though I think I didn't do my best
As I wait impatiently at my desk
Waiting for the results from my test
Did I do badly or did I do good?
I really hate the chance I might get booed
And while I wait, high in fear
I think I'd rather kill myself with a beer
And all of a sudden, I see in front of me
A time machine, oh no, I feel strangely green
So I step inside, unsure what to do
But press a button saying '50 minutes ago'
Finally the journey ends sat in my seat
The test in front of me, so I'm ready to repeat
And when I'm done, the teacher collects
My paper and the rest of the tests
So I get up and ask how I've done
And the teacher looks at me like a bad son
'Your answers are wrong, you horrible pest!'
Oh dear, I think I failed that test.

Tiziano Cafaro (14)
St Ninian's High School, Glasgow

Good Times, Great Memories, My Papa

My wee papa, I miss him every day
We had a great time on holiday

When he died I was so upset
He hadn't even reached sixty yet

When his coffin was taken away
I burst into tears straight away

My wee papa was a funny guy
I didn't really think that he would die

When I realised he was gone forever
All I wanted to do was cry a river

The day before he died we watched Celtic play
They won 3-0, we had a great day

He loved to watch the green and white play
They were perfect in every way

So now my papa is up in the sky
In my heart he will never die.

Aaron McCaig (14)
St Ninian's High School, Glasgow

Untitled

Good old times with my grandad
He went out of his way
To see me every day
Old but wise
He would pick me up with surprise.

I loved him so much
He had the magic touch
He even cleaned out my rabbit hutch.

He took me to the park
With my ball
He couldn't run at all
Because he was too small.

I liked going to the shops with him
To see his good mate, Jim
He also taught me how to swim
That's why I loved him.

He had funny hair
He had a lift to take him up the stair.

I miss him so much
I wish I could bring him back
With his magic touch.

Sean Pittner (14)
St Ninian's High School, Glasgow

Living With Word Blindness

Can't read, can't write
What is up with me?
People laugh, people stare
They think I am stupid
But I am not.

I get scared, I get worried
I get nervous and I get shaky
Especially when I read and write
The words seem to get all jumbled up.

The days go by, some better, some worse
But somehow I always manage
I try to think of positive things
To make me feel quite happy.

A job interview is hard for me
Because I can't read or write well
I always do my very best
To impress them nevertheless.

I am really good at other things
Like football, tennis and cricket
So after all, it's not so bad
Even if I am dyslexic.

Jennifer Lynn (13)
St Ninian's High School, Glasgow

The Goldfish Bowl

When I look out through the glass,
All I see is a vision of you and a vision of me.

People scampering everywhere,
Some here, some there,
TV blaring all the time,
Can't wait for the lights to go out,
Wish it was nine.

The lid is opened, my food is dropped,
I have to swim all the way to the top.
I swim back down to the stony bed,
I swim to a leaf and rest my head.

I wake up with a fright,
Someone has just switched on a light.
Children screaming, laughing aloud,
Coming and going from the maddening crowd.

People are giants compared to me,
I don't belong here, I should be in the sea.
They look at me with glaring faces,
Tapping on the glass with mischievous graces.

But who is in the goldfish bowl?
Is it you or me?
Who is imprisoned in the world they call free.

Lauren Cherry (13)
St Ninian's High School, Glasgow

Good Times, Great Memories

Little white dresses
In a big shop
But the dress I wanted
Was at the very top.

Spectacular sparkling jewels
Also with little white mules.

It was my big day
I began to pray.

I was nervous
About this service.

Photos getting taken everywhere
I felt like everyone wanted to stare.

Finally the mass was over
The party was about to begin
Everybody stood up and started to sing.

Presents piling high
Almost as if they were going
To go into the sky.

A memory forever
I won't forget - never ever
Memories to treasure
It was a pleasure.

Jasmine Meek (14)
St Ninian's High School, Glasgow

Religion

Religion is like a stranger
You don't know what's before, you don't know
What's after
Like Jesus in His manger
And the three strangers who came after.

Religion is to be cared for
Something to be shared for
No matter what you do
Your faith will follow you

Adam and Eve may have been bare
It's a shame that snake was there
Adam was the one who was tough
Until he fell in love

But it's not great from lies
Full of fantasies created on love, all lies
It's full of warfare and cries
Causes destruction because of lies

Pitchforks and fire, Satan's desire
Here we are, land of fear and fire
Six, six, six, the number on its head
The lives of sinners are soon to end.

Patrick Coll (15)
St Ninian's High School, Glasgow

Through The Eyes Of A Whale

Through the eyes of a whale,
I began to see how horrible it would be,
If we carry on our killing spree,
Using nets and hooks,
Never setting it free
And if it manages to escape,
We will shoot it down with our guns,
It cries in pain, we don't give a damn,
I wonder what it would feel like to be a helpless whale.

Deep in the sea I am swimming free,
Watching all the fish as they swim by me,
Also the sharks, the dolphins, the sea horses and crabs,
Lobsters, squid, jellyfish and starfish.
Then suddenly, nets appear
And then one goes for me, but it misses.
I swim and swim as fast as I can,
Dodging nets as they take out their harpoons
And fire at me as if I am their enemy.
I cannot give up, but then it hits me,
I am trapped in the net, the harpoon hit me,
I am caught like a prisoner in a jail,
Helpless and lonely.

Andrew Dickson (12)
St Ninian's High School, Glasgow

Cara's Eyes

Looking through Cara's eyes
The world seems such a surprise.

The snow had fallen softly on the ground
It was time to go out and run around.

The snow felt fresh, new and clean
Her reflection gave off a sparkling gleam.

The world was quiet, not a single sound
She suddenly realised no one was around.

She began to feel lonely and cold inside
She wished someone was by her side.

Tears leaked down her beautiful face
Her tummy was rumbling at such a pace.

Then out of nowhere a whistle came
Someone was calling Cara by her name.

Now that Cara is safe at home
Her owner is now going to give her a bone.

Amy Gallacher (13)
St Ninian's High School, Glasgow

Give A Voice To Someone Who Can't Speak

I can see, I can hear, I can walk,
I just can't talk.

I can't speak my feelings or tell someone a story,
I can't watch a film and say, 'Oh, that's gory!'

I feel so angry and upset,
That I am cooped up just like a pet.

Why me? Did I do something wrong?
This has gone on for too long.

I feel excruciating pain,
I can't go outside and play any games.

My doctors can't do anything about it,
Mum's even tried her emergency kit.

My family and I have done everything together,
It looks like it's stuck with me forever.

I can see, I can hear, I can walk,
I just can't talk!

Nicole McSporran (13)
St Ninian's High School, Glasgow

Living On The Street

My name is Pete
I live on the street
The street is a wonderful place

I have no money
But I'm very funny
The street is a wonderful place

I have to steal
To make my meal
The street is a wonderful place

I sing and dance
To get a laugh
The street is a wonderful place

When the skies open
I get a soaking
The street is a wonderful place

I'm very sick
Now I've got to pick between life or death
I've got to get some money
Or be very funny
The street is a confusing place

I choose to be funny
So I have no money
The street is a wonderful place

My heart stops beating
Now I'm not speaking
The street is a horrible place.

Christopher Paul (13)
St Ninian's High School, Glasgow

Sister

Love is a very special thing,
With all the intensity it may bring.
You are fair and I am dark,
Though our beliefs aren't so far apart.
You have a girl and I have boy,
And to our hearts they bring us joy.
You will kiss and lovingly embrace,
While this emotion I'd rather not face.
You, my sister, are very sensitive,
But I am so demonstrative.
I lie and pray to God at night,
That all your life you'll be alright.
I know sometimes I can be moody
And other times you can be broody,
But if I ever had to choose,
You I hope I'll never lose.

Jordan Elliot Kelly (12)
St Ninian's High School, Glasgow

Untitled

Humans are stupid
I wag my tail and bark
But they do nothing

Humans are stupid
I scratch the door and stare
But they do nothing

Humans are stupid
I run round in circles crying
But they do nothing

Humans are stupid
Can't they see I just need a pee?

Andrew Miller (13)
St Ninian's High School, Glasgow

Away With Words

Galloping softly on the golden sand
Wild and free on my land
No one dared to battle me
As I was fierce and worry-free
Standing proud as the leader of my pack
Until the day I would never go back

I was out in the field one night
Until my herd went out of sight
I heard something strange, but nothing was there
Until my eyes fell into a stare
I turned around, but it was too late
I was stuck to the ground like a wooden crate

With ropes on my legs, body and head
At that moment I would have rather been dead
Before I knew it, I was in a stable all cosy and warm
Locked out from that hideous storm
But it didn't change the fact I wanted to go
Go home where the blue winds blow.

Brie Friel (12)
St Ninian's High School, Glasgow

Looking At The World Through Someone Else's Eyes

I see a hobo out on the street
He trips up on my feet
I say sorry and so does he
He walks away, nowhere to go
I'm late for work, I need to go.

I wonder what he'll do today
Wander the streets or beg for change?
Looking through his eyes
Life must be sad.

How did he get there?
What did he do?
Was drink the problem?
Or even drugs too?
How can I help him?
What can I do?
I can't do anything,
I need help too.

Lewis Morton (13)
St Ninian's High School, Glasgow

In The Zoo

Behind my bars, all the tall creatures watching me
I can't even swing about without them
Tall beasts give me peace
At least they're not ferocious
They swarm about you
Like a swarm of locusts.

Oh no, not the younger beasts
Come on, just give peace
All my friends swinging with me
They all wish they could disappear
That would be fun
At least my big grey, long-nosed friend can steal their buns.

Now it's night, good, they've gone
Now we can have our food
There's not a noise
Except for my big grey friend
They'll be back, the beasts.

Even us monkeys need some sleep
We're not banana-munching creeps
The zoo all quiet, it's time to rest
We're the best.

Stuart McEwan (13)
St Ninian's High School, Glasgow

Blind World

The grass is green,
The sky is blue,
The sun is yellow,
If only I knew.

Why am I blind?
Oh, why can't I see,
A bus, a car,
Or even a tree?

When I'm walking around I hear,
All different sounds,
Children laughing, dogs barking,
At the merry-go-round.

Why am I blind?
Oh, why can't I see,
The beautiful world,
That's all around me?

Yet I know there's a reason
For me being blind,
That's the one thing,
That I need to find.

Katy Graham (13)
St Ninian's High School, Glasgow

Bullying

I was shaking like a leaf
As I started to pick up the pace
My palms were sweating
I could taste salty tears running down my face.

My pulse was getting faster
My heart was pounding out of my chest
I could hear people laughing at me as I lay on the ground
I could feel a blinding pain in my stomach
As if someone had kicked me.

I was petrified to say anything
I felt as weak as a child
I could hear her evil voice going through my head
I was terrified with all the threats.

My life was shattering to pieces
I could feel the earth getting closer and closer
I could hear her voice in my sleep
I just wanted to cut myself deep.

I need someone to turn to
But no one was there to help me
I felt as if I had no voice
I just wanted to ask a few questions
Why me, what have I done?
I am just the same as anyone
Or aren't I?

Martine Lennox (13)
St Ninian's High School, Glasgow

The Teacher's Eyes Through Mine

Same old faces at the front,
I look at them and start to grunt.
I say to them to come over here,
So I can shout and bawl in their ear.

They look at me really terrified,
But the reason for punishment was not verified.
I called the headmaster,
He couldn't get there any faster.

The troublemakers turned pale,
As if they were going to jail.
The rebels were suspended,
As I had intended.

They were escorted out,
Without a doubt,
And the class said,
'What was that all about?'

Michael Watson (13)
St Ninian's High School, Glasgow

My Sister

My sister is a selfish child
And she is really wild.
She is as thick as a donkey,
She has my mum and dad wrapped around her little finger.
My sister is good at gymnastics,
And her body is like elastic.
She can dance, she can sing
Like an artist on a skating rink.
Even though she is all that,
She is my sister and I love her.

Saba Sarwar (12)
St Ninian's High School, Glasgow

Extra Time

Extra time and I am worried
I went in for that tackle, I really hurried
I swiped for the ball as if I didn't care
The look of my team makes me scared
After all, I scored an own goal
I wish I was swallowed by a big, dark hole
I realise now what I have done
I have made the score 2-1
All I hear are people cries
Try seeing it through my own eyes
My manager shakes his head in despair
I hope he knows I really care
I feel as if I am a disgrace
You can tell by my face
The crowd looked on, shocked and surprised
Try seeing it through their own eyes.

Jack Hinton (13)
St Ninian's High School, Glasgow

Away With Words

Day in, day out
Thirty faces staring back at me.
I'm exhausted and frustrated,
I feel like I'm going to burst.

Each day they come in,
Wondering what they're going to be doing,
If they will be talking or writing,
Because I can't be bothered teaching them.

They probably talk about me,
But I don't care.
I sit in my classroom,
Just getting on with my life.
Then fifty-five minutes go by
And another thirty faces come in.

Mary-Jane McPhee (13)
St Ninian's High School, Glasgow

Great Memories

M emories, memories
E xciting memories
M y youngest cousin, Darlene
O pened her eyes bright and shimmering
R ight and left she looked at me
I ntelligent is seen in her
E nergetic like a monkey, she dances on a podium
S he is a parrot that shouts in our ears.

She jumps up high
And can reach the sky
She shouts out loud
But I cannot do that up to the cloud
We play all day and night
We don't notice that the moon glows too bright
She is not only my cousin
But she is also my best friend and my life.

Manrica Sese (12)
St Ninian's High School, Glasgow

Untitled

It is hard for me
To tell you that I love you
When I am standing over your grave.

As I lie in my bed
Thinking why God would do this to me
I start to cry
My world is nothing without you.

I need to have you here with me
To hold me, to kiss me
Maybe if I try, you'll come back.

It hurts so much to know you're dead
I can never let it go inside
That is why I try to die
To be with you.

Amy Johnstone (12)
St Ninian's High School, Glasgow

Tree

I have been here since the dawn of time.
I have watched the world grow up,
Seen the days turn into night,
Blanketed into darkness.

I remember when I was a mere sapling,
Bark as brown as a muddy dog,
Leaves like almond-shaped emeralds.
A small tree in a forest of wood.

Then the men came,
Axes in hand, saws in arm.
If we had had legs, we would have fled.
They took us one by one.

We were sawn down into strips,
Penned on by young and old,
Sent from here to there,
Transferred from eye to brain.

I see the people every day,
They seem to tower above me.
I, the one who witnessed Culloden,
I, who once towered above them.

Eventually they threw me out,
Littered me onto hard ground,
Amongst the sweet wrappers and cigarettes,
They stank of death, decay, disease.

I became soil, brown and earthy.
Tree seeds rained down upon me,
I became one with them.

Now I stand tall,
A mighty tree in a forest of wood.

Natasha Caven (12)
St Ninian's High School, Glasgow

Squad Of Loyalty

It was quiet, too quiet
Like the calm before a riot
In the boats we waited with our guns
Knowing that when we hit the beach, we would have to run.

The thought of when we hit the beach, bullets would start to fly
And my friends, my unit, my team, my squad
That some would have to die
We hit the beach and started to use our heads
We would let the enemy pass and pretend we were already dead.

It was a good plan but that wasn't the case
The enemy pulled out their guns and started to pick up the pace
My heart started to beat as fast as it would
I would have picked up my gun if only I could.

There was a sharp pain in my thigh
I was shot and about to die
But I pulled up the strength to pick up a gun
But unfortunately, the ammo was done.

A man came over and shot me in the head
My unit escaped, but I am dead
Some ran away, others stayed brave
But all were made to dig their own grave.

Some took a jump, others a dive
It didn't matter, they were getting buried alive
My friends in my unit added up to ten
Now in Heaven we are reunited again.

Andrew Allan (13)
St Ninian's High School, Glasgow

Turn Back Time

I would change school subjects and tests
They are the things I most detest

I would also change the weather to snow
That's the way I want it to go

I would change my back garden to a swimming pool
Then I would be cool and not a fool

I would change nearly every single rule
They are all certainly not very cool

I would change my family so we were rich
The thing I would buy would be a football pitch

I would change all cars so they were good
If they were so good they might serve food

I've kept this to last
This is the thing I would mostly change in the past

I would change all the shops to sweet shops
So my mum couldn't buy cleaning stuff such as mops.

Ross Gunning (12)
St Ninian's High School, Glasgow

The Abandoned Dog

He is left outside alone in the rain,
Poor dog is in so much pain.
He moans and cries like a tiger stepping on a trap,
So lost and lonely, wishing he had a map!
Sorrowful he is, he feels he has no heart.
It is like someone is using him as a dart.

People shout, 'He is a pig,'
And shoo him away for stealing a twig.
His fur is a piece of dirt,
When people shout, 'Horrid thing!'
It makes him rather hurt.

He smells like a pile of trash,
And sometimes he is lucky to find a bit of cash.
He looks like a skeleton,
As he walks down the street called Helleton.
One day he will find someone to love him for all his days,
But right now in the street he lays.
Now the sorrowful dog is never to be seen,
Because the people in the street are so mean.

Melissa Stead (12)
St Ninian's High School, Glasgow

The Bully

I was standing at the school gate
The bully came up to me
I was shaking like a leaf.

He smacked me in the face
I fell to the ground
He picked me back up.

The bully punched me on the nose
The thick red blood was running down my face
I felt excruciating pain.

Then the bully picked me up
And threw me against a wall
My head smacked on it and I fell to the ground.

The bully laughed and walked away
I thought to myself, *why me?*
I am just the same as everyone else.
Or am I?

Robert Campbell (13)
St Ninian's High School, Glasgow

Spirit Of The Horse

Galloping free in open land
Strong and proud, is the way they'll stand.
Lovely coat so shiny and bay
Long black mane all covered in hay.
A sunny day trotting in the sand
Leap for a jump, over and land.
The sound of the hooves as they gallop around
It may be loud but I love that sound.
Shoes shining in the sun
Mane blowing in the wind, just having fun.
When they're hungry, they will kick the door
Just give them some hay, then give them some more.
Crunch, crunch, crunch, as they eat the hay
Yum, yum, yum, is the word they'll say.
If its bay, if it's black, if it's grey, if it's dun
A pretty little pony, there to have fun.
Having a pony is such a treasure
Having a pony is a love you can't measure.

Simone Barrett (12)
St Ninian's High School, Glasgow

Vend

(Or how I learnt to start worrying and love Toffee Crisp bars)

Beach balls in the boot
Bairns in the back
Off I go into the duty-free
To get a good snack.

I cornered the vending machine
And got out my change
Then I chose a Toffee Crisp
From the very extensive range.

I put in 75p
K-chik

. . .

Nothing happened.

I thumped the little blighter
And with a great big slam
Then I started shouting . . .
'Oh no! Oh dear! Oh damn!'

And then I saw a wrapper
Shining brown and gold
The choc bar fell on my napper
And it was finally sold!

Now I have my Toffee Crisp
In all its chewy glory!
And I hope others don't go through
This exact same story.

Jordan Campbell (12)
St Ninian's High School, Glasgow

Away With Words

I wonder what it would be like to get bullied all day
Not being able to learn or even to play
With teeth like splinters
And breath like sick
The bullies never get tired of poor old Mick

So here he comes acting all big and cool
And he makes poor Mick look like a fool
The bully has a face that could frighten a bear
Believe you me, he is a real scare

And the tears fall from poor Mick's eyes
So upset about a pile of lies
By now his face is scarlet-red
I bet he wishes now that he was dead

But it changes now that the story is told
And now that we are all 40 years old
The bully grew up and now lives on the street
And struggles to find something to eat

But the same could not be said for Mick
Now he's mega rich and super slick
He still remembers his awful school years
When he was always reduced to tears
But that is the past and out of sight
And now the future is looking bright.

Danny Hale (12)
St Ninian's High School, Glasgow

Bullies

Bullies are sneaky and tricky
As teachers are smart,
Teachers look after you
As though you are a work of art!

Bullies are cowards,
Who lurk in the park,
They have no morals,
You know they'll be there tomorrow.

Pushing and threatening,
Hurling verbal abuse,
Day or night they have no use.

They like to hurt people less obvious than themselves,
Thinking they're smart, but really they're miles apart.
They're the cowards, but no one can see the damage they do,
Not only today, but a lifetime through.

How would it feel if there were no bullies at school?
Pupils would be relaxed and teachers could be cool.
Rid the bullies, rid the pain,
Let us have our freedom again.
The pupils would be happy,
The teachers less snappy,
Oh, what a cool school it would be!

Ryan Pirnie (12)
St Ninian's High School, Glasgow

Salmon

Salmon, salmon, down the stream,
They look like multicoloured jelly beans
And they all have the same dream,
To join their friends up the stream,
Avoiding the bears and their claws,
Jumping over rivers and logs.
Some are yellow, some are green,
Slipping out of the bears' claws,
Waiting for that glimpse of that magical waterfall.

If a bear caught one,
Its teeth would go through it like a chainsaw with wood,
Slicing and dicing like a true bear should.
Tug, tug, a tug on my rod,
On the hook a beautiful salmon.
The poor big soul there in all its glory,
I can't wait to tell my friends this wonderful story.

Matthew Cassidy (12)
St Ninian's High School, Glasgow

Golden Yesterdays

It was fun when I was in primary one
Work was easy
Cutting and pasting and plenty of time wasting.

Running in the playground, fun and games
And calling each other silly names
PE was good
So was the lunchtime food.

Trips and projects were fun to do
In art I drew a shoe
Lots of friends I had there
I still wish I could be in primary one
Things now are not much fun.

Liam Finn (13)
St Thomas Aquinas RC Secondary School, Glasgow

Neon City

Neon city is like Glasgow at night,
With all of the very fancy lights.
From my house it's a wonderful sight,
Because I live up seventeen flights of stairs in a massive flat,
So tell me, what do you think of that?

Loads of people go to pubs or casinos,
Mostly always dressed up in tuxedos.
The reason they go is because the pubs look good,
Or maybe it's cos they get loads of food.

The thing I really, really hate,
Is when at night I'm wide awake.
And all of these drunken guys
Are always punching each other in the eyes.

And when I get up in the morning,
Every two minutes I'm always yawning
Because I could not get to sleep,
So I tried the old, 'count the sheep'.

Eventually I got to shut my eyes
And neon city has gone . . . bye-bye!
Maybe these neon lights
Will come some other wonderful night.

Marc Ainsworth (13)
St Thomas Aquinas RC Secondary School, Glasgow

Things In The Bin

A grotty fish head from last week
One bottle of bad milk with yellow chunks in it
Sticky brown banana skins
A half-eaten, mouldy, smelly tuna sandwich
The odd chewed-up pen lid
A rotten, half-decaying plastic arm
The most disgusting bloodstained tissue ever.

Ross Nolan (13)
St Thomas Aquinas RC Secondary School, Glasgow

The Fight

Have to learn how to skip
Can't stop, won't stop
Better watch I don't trip
Can't even go to the shop

Time for the punch bag
So get your punch mitts
Let's beat this bag till it's an old rag
Let's see how many hits you can get in two minutes

Tonight's the night
Let's get ready
For the night of the big fight
The person you are fighting is called Freddie

Jab, jab, keep throwing them jabs
Give him a good right hook
Play fair, don't grab
Nae luck, pal, looks like it's back to the book.

Craig Goodall (13)
St Thomas Aquinas RC Secondary School, Glasgow

Memories In My Mum's Heart

Michael smiling when he was fit and well
Sharing chips from the chippy
Arguing over spilt tea
Holding hands and walking in the park
Holding hands on his hospital bed
Life support machines bleeping for help
Feeling helpless as his life fades away
Missing him more day by day.

Jennifer McGilligan (13)
St Thomas Aquinas RC Secondary School, Glasgow

Watching The World Go By

Sitting by the window
People rushing by
They look like little ants
I feel I want to cry.

Why can't I be out with them?
I'm sitting here alone
In this quiet hospital
I remember when my skin had tone.

I can never sleep at night
The beds are so hard
I loved my old one
At least it's not like card.

I want to see my family
I miss them tons
I want my house back
And my wife's home-made buns.

Sitting by the window
As life goes past
I think it's time I went to bed
Before tomorrow comes in too fast.

Amy Brennan (13)
St Thomas Aquinas RC Secondary School, Glasgow

Golden Yesterdays

(Poem for Daniel)

Sister and brother,
Brother and sister.
Big strong brother
And small cute sister.

Fighting and laughing,
Laughing and fighting.
We cheered each other up
In thunder and lightning.

Sharing secrets,
Laughing and joking,
That was before you started smoking!

It was me and you,
You and me,
That's the way I thought it would always be.

We're growing up now,
I now see,
But remember, bro,
I have you and you'll always have me.

Yes, oh yes, those days were a buzz,
We knew no one was better than us.

Melanie Wood (13)
St Thomas Aquinas RC Secondary School, Glasgow

Golden Yesterdays

She used to help me with my maths
And when I was sore,
But now she's gone,
There is no more.

I wonder, I wonder
If she will ever come back,
She used to make me cards
When I was upset.

She hugged and kissed me
When she was poorly
And now I am lonely.

I wonder, I wonder
What was going on?
My mum walked in
And said no more.

Fiona Neil (13)
St Thomas Aquinas RC Secondary School, Glasgow

Golden Yesterdays

My mum and dad are the best
I love them very much

They let me play all day and night
And do whatever I want

I fall on the ground
They pick me up and make it all better

I miss that so, so much
I would give back so much to do that one more time.

John Paul Gillan (13)
St Thomas Aquinas RC Secondary School, Glasgow

Watching The World Go By

As I watch the world go by
I don't mean to gawp or stare
I just feel lonely
And want some company

Although I am alone in this big, big place
I feel I am missing something
A friend maybe

I only want to talk
Have some tea and ask them how they have been
What I have done in the past, I didn't mean
If I could go back I would

As the years go by, I feel even lonelier
But I can't do much as I am older
Being alone isn't so bad
Although when I am, I do feel sad

I have always wanted a friend
And although my time is near
I don't think I could adapt to life outside
As I am not just a prisoner in here, but in my mind too
All I have is my cell
And the clothes on my back
As I look out of my bars and watch the world go by.

Ryan Connelly (14)
St Thomas Aquinas RC Secondary School, Glasgow

Golden Yesterdays

I had a dream last night
Going back to the old days
So much of life to explore
The world was like a maze

So many toys to play with
So much fun I had
I'll let you in on a little secret
I was kind of bad

My dad would say I could get away with murder
It's true, but I liked it so much
I remember my mum would say
I break everything I touch

Now I've told you what I was like
You could say I was a little crazy
Those were the best days of my life
But now I am too bored and lazy.

Ryan Glencross (13)
St Thomas Aquinas RC Secondary School, Glasgow

Golden Yesterday

My mum looked back on the times we had
Even the times I was sad

My mum has been proud since primary one
Even when she saw the trophy I never won

When I go and see my dad
It reminds me of the times I could have had.

Simon Mulholland (13)
St Thomas Aquinas RC Secondary School, Glasgow

Golden Years

My grandfather is gone,
But somehow we stay strong.
How do we go on without him?

Even though my granny's still here,
Every moment is dear.
For what will we do without her?

She has to move home,
But where shall I roam,
When I have to go on without her?

We've always been able,
To put food on the table,
But what will it be like without them?

We will be sad,
Especially Dad,
When we all have to go on without them.

Rois Porter (13)
St Thomas Aquinas RC Secondary School, Glasgow

Things Under A Bed!

Boxes full of pictures and all their memories.
Packet of pickled onion crisps stinking out the room.
Old shoes that I have lost and have been looking for.
Earrings and jewellery that I lost the other day.
Receipts from last year.
Crumbs, fluff and hair, all stuck to the carpet.
An old diary full of secrets.
A horrible napkin full of tears.

Samantha Gilroy (13)
St Thomas Aquinas RC Secondary School, Glasgow

Aberdeen

Train journey
Two and a half hours long
Cramp in my legs
Could only say
'Aberdeen'
Home sweet home

So happy
To see
My hometown
'Aberdeen'

Smelling the air
Fabulous

People were rushing
Pushing their trolleys
I just dawdled
Didn't need to rush

Aberdeen is mine
Always will be
It won't move
Always be there

'Aberdeen'.

Julie MacDonald (15)
Snowdon School, Stirling

Like A Bird In The Sky

Birds in the sky
Wish I could fly
Up there so high
Like a bird
In the sky

Soaring higher
And higher
Up with the stars
Beside Mars

Living in a nest
Feeding the chicks
Teaching them to fly
Like a bird
In the sky

Finding food
Keeping out
Of danger
Wish I could be
Just like them

Like a bird in the sky
I wish I could fly.

Leanne McKay (15)
Snowdon School, Stirling

In The Care Homes

In care
All you want to do
Is go home
But every time you ask
Your social worker says
It's out of their hands now
All you want to do
Is run away

All the time to think
About running away
Sometimes you do
Sometimes you don't

But running away
Doesn't get you anywhere
It only gets you
One more step away
From staying at home
And one step closer
To secure

Every time you go to a panel
You want to sit next to
Your mum and dad
When the panel says
You're not getting home
For a while
You turn to look at your mum
And see her breaking
Inside.

Nikki Inglis (14)
Snowdon School, Stirling

Down South

Down south
At the caravan park
Keeran fell out
The door

Phone rang
Answer said Gran
Uncle Tony said
Put me on
To Gran

Keeran is OK
Gran said
Call it a day
Grandad said

Let's go back
Let's go home
Uncle Tony
Is all alone.

Natasha Todd (15)
Snowdon School, Stirling

Still Waters Run Deep

Deeper than the sea
Deeper than your dreams
The deepest thing
Is a woman's heart
Deeper than the world
Deep like the ocean
Deeper than emotion
Deeper than devotion
Deepest thing of all
Is a woman's heart.

Ashleigh Green (16)
Snowdon School, Stirling

Blackpool

I remember a time
When I was ten
Went to Blackpool
With Mum and Dad

Easter time
So exciting
Pleasure Beach
All the rides

Ice Blast
So scared
Pepsi Max
Stomach churns
Revolution
Fantastic

Went to Blackpool
Aged fifteen
Nothing changed
Great place.

Eve Butterworth (15)
Snowdon School, Stirling

America

America
1997 turning seven
The sky, the day
Lasted forever

America
Purple Barbie dress
3-piece Barbie
Ice cream cake
Chucky Cheese
My favourite place

America
Brand new clothes
Beauty parlour
To get pampered

America
New school
New friends
1997 turning seven.

Andrea Raeburn (16)
Snowdon School, Stirling

Residential Kid

Residential kid
Shouting
Screaming
Running

You miss home
You have your friends
Your enemies

You wait a week
To go home again
You go to school
Watch the clock
Pass by

You have good times
And bad
Nothing's great
Until you're home

Residential kid
Laughing
Learning
Going on trips
Cinema
Skating

People listen
To you
Help with your problems
Take your point
Of view.

Tammy Walker (15)
Snowdon School, Stirling

Christmas Eve

Christmas Eve
About six years old
Mum was cooking
My dinner

Waiting for Dad
To come and see me
It wasn't snowing
Really wanted it to

Just liked to play
In the snow

About eight o'clock
Dad came to the door
It was snowing!
I was so happy

In the back garden
We made snow angels
And had snowball fights
I remember I had so much fun
With my dad

He told me to get my stuff
I was staying with him
Made me even more happy
We stopped off at the shop
And bought Christmas DVDs

On Christmas Eve.

Natalie Robertson (13)
Snowdon School, Stirling

Becoming A Teenager

13th birthday party
Growing up fast
Lots of friends
At school

Planned for ages
Parents wanted
A special day
Dad built outdoor pool
For the grand
Occasion

Night before
Everything ready
Music system up
The food
The cake
Everything

Being thirteen
Felt good
Not young anymore
Young adulthood.

Erin Peters (15)
Snowdon School, Stirling

I Remember

I remember
When I was little
Moved to Garthdee

The sun
Was really shining
The breeze
Blew past me

I remember
With my mum
Went to the shops

Came back
Da was cutting
The grass
The smell was lovely

I still remember
That smell
The bright sunshine
I felt so happy

So happy . . .

Gillian Morgan (14)
Snowdon School, Stirling

Blackpool Trip

Blackpool trip
With staff and girls
Sun was shining
Sky was bright

First ride
Ice Blast
Best ride
At Blackpool
Cool

Went on the shows
On the arcades
Lunch at the mini bus
Burger King for tea

Trip to Blackpool
It's the place
For me
Blackpool
Cool.

Natalie Stewart (15)
Snowdon School, Stirling

Poems

If you give me a book
About English
I'll do spelling
I'll read it
But I can't write
A poem

I'm like a book
A book you can't open
A book that stays closed
You can't read me
The pages inside me
They just don't get read

I like songs
If it's rock
It sometimes makes me angry
If it's slow
It sometimes makes me sad
Music is the way
I express myself.

Suzanne Casey (14)
Snowdon School, Stirling

My Team

Went to Easter Road
Football stadium
Celtic Hibs game
Felt excited
Sitting there in the cold
Waiting for the game
To start

Went with my cousin, Zander
Really want Celtic
To win

Amazing seeing
The footballers play
Cheering when Celtic
Scored

Half time
Celtic 2 Hibs 1
Second half
They won!

So proud
To see my team
Win.

Catherine Watson (15)
Snowdon School, Stirling

War

Footsteps
Blood lying corpses in the
Mud
Bullets lying on the ground
Hear the screams of people all around
Children screaming 'Help
Me please'
Begging on their knees
Men running from
The fight
Slowly dropping
In your sight
Being shot in cold blood
Lying dead in the mud
Beaten and slashed
Shot and burnt
Why do we have
An evil world?
Can't we live in
Peace?
And stop this war
Between one race.

Kimberley Rushton (14)
Snowdon School, Stirling

Ma Dug

There's big dugs
Wee dugs
Middle size dugs
Collies, terriers and retrievers
But the one dug that fits fur me
Is ma wee terrier

She barks aw day
She barks aw night
Likes ta pit up
A hefty fight

She sleeps aw day
She sleeps aw night
Thinking o the bone
She ate yesterday night

Dreemin aboot cats and that
Worryin that she might
Get fat
Butchers fur breakfast
Bakers fur tea
My God
Ma dug
Eats better than me!

Sueanna Stronnach (15)
Snowdon School, Stirling

At My Cousin's

Eight years old
Went to my cousin
Leona
First time
I met her

Me and my cousin
Went in the garden
A sunny day
Smell of flowers
Nice strong smell

Played houses
With my cousin
Birds in the sky
Beautiful shiny blue
Glittery sky.

Nadine Wilson (13)
Snowdon School, Stirling

Falling Out

Friends always fall out
You're all alone with nobody
Left out by mates
And lonely also
In school people laugh
Never felt so stupid
Getting secrets passed around
Face as red as a tomato
Nobody to chat to or listen to
You're the most sad person in school.

Elli Williams (12)
The Community School of Auchterarder, Auchterarder

My Grangran

I'm sitting there
In my class
I'm sitting there
I wish time would pass

I can't wait to see her
I just can't wait to go home
I can't wait to see her
Maybe first I should phone

The bell's just gone
I'm grabbing my book
The bell's just gone
I'm getting my jacket off the hook

I'm nearly home
I'm racing across the road
I'm nearly home
Oops! I nearly stepped on a toad

Finally I'm home
I call her name
Finally I'm home
I want to play a game

My mum comes up to me
With a sad look on her face
My mum comes up to me
While I'm untying my lace

She tells me the problem
I burst into tears
She tells me the problem
One of my biggest fears

My grangran's gone now
And I miss her so much.

Mariea Turner (12)
The Community School of Auchterarder, Auchterarder

Grade 3 Cello

The day had finally arrived
When I was doing my grade
I was feeling so nervous
That the bow was shaking the strings

The examiner sat there watching
When I was playing my pieces
My teacher was accompanying me
As I stringed along

When I had finished my pieces
My teacher left the room
I started to play my scales
That I had endlessly revised

The minutes crawled by like hours
While I did the aural test
Singing all the notes she played
And clapping all the beats

When the examiner stood up
And walked over to her desk
I could feel my hands shaking
As I was now facing a book

The page had lots of pieces
All were for doing sight reading
She said I had 30 seconds
To look and play away

When it was finally over
I had to go back to school
And now a few months later
I'm glad to say I passed.

Emma Kelman (12)
The Community School of Auchterarder, Auchterarder

The Easter Poem

At the supper, when everyone gathered around Jesus,
He had things to say to all of us.
He said, 'Take this bread as My body,'
Then everyone nodded.
Then He said, 'Take this wine as My blood.'
Then everybody thought that His love would flood.
Later that evening, He disappeared to die for us,
This is the love of Jesus.
The next day it was hell for everyone,
And there was no happiness for anyone.
As Jesus laid on the Cross,
Everyone thought that His life was lost.
As the dark nails went through His wrists,
This was the power of the Jew's fists.
As the Cross stood on the ground,
Everyone saw Him in a bound.
The next day, the town was quiet,
In Heaven, God wasn't in a riot.
As they put Jesus in the stone grave,
When Jesus was alive, He was brave.
As they rolled the round, stone door over the entrance,
The Jews were not filled with repentance.
Later on Mary passed by,
She was miserable because Jesus had died.
Then she looked at the grave, the door was open.
She was confused, so she went in.
Then she thought, *my Son has died for us.*
Then standing in front of her was Jesus.

Douglas Rees (12)
The Community School of Auchterarder, Auchterarder

My Grandma

Today I knew it was the day
The day I was going to my grandma's house

My mum drove up the long, narrow street
Turning left then right and right again
Till there was a sudden stop
My heart was racing with excitement

The jingling bells of the house door opening
There she stood by the gate
With her smiley face
I knew it was going to be a great day

She greeted me and sat me down
She sang songs to me
And I tried to sing along

We told jokes to each other
How she laughed at them
I had a happy, glowing feeling inside

Then I saw the car go by
It was my mum
I stepped outside once again
And said goodbye

I was so sad
But then she said
'You'll be back tomorrow'
Then I was so happy.

Amy Byrne (12)
The Community School of Auchterarder, Auchterarder

Secondary School

The first day of secondary school has come,
Butterflies in my stomach,
So many people,
Some so tall
And some so small.

As I walked towards a group of people,
My heart thumped,
They were so nice to me though,
So there was nothing for me to worry about.

They have done so much for me now,
My primary friends were nothing like my friends now,
So it's like the world's turned round for me.

Now we are the best of friends.

Lauren Riva (12)
The Community School of Auchterarder, Auchterarder

My Granny

My granny is sweet fudge
Always with a smile on her face
Kind and always ready for a cuddle

Her short, curly, brown hair
Her voice is like a bird
Her eyes are twinkling stars

My granny is as wise as an owl
She is as funny as a joker
As reliable as the sun on a sunny day

She nurtures her plants like she did with me
There is always a smell of freshly baked goodies
She treats everyone like she wants them to treat her.

Kelly MacLaren (12)
The Community School of Auchterarder, Auchterarder

I Like . . .

I like playing football.
I like kicking the ball into the back of the net,
Scoring all the important goals,
Being the man of the match,
I like everyone round me cheering my name.

I like playing hide-and-seek.
Running away from the catcher,
Chasing after people,
Getting the best hiding places.

I like playing basketball.
Taking long rangers,
Scoring two or three pointers,
The sound of the ball going through the net,
The sound of the whistle going when we score.

I like going out with my mates.
Messing about with them,
I like going places with them.

Josh Goold (12)
The Community School of Auchterarder, Auchterarder

Snow, What Fun

I sat in the classroom, sitting and waiting for the bell,
Then after fifty-four tiring minutes, it finally went,
The uproar to get outside in the snow.

Down on the Astroturf, the place to be,
Like Heaven for the people who want some fun,
For the laughs and the fun where people run.

Running through the white sheet,
Like a clear horizon on a cold winter's day,
Having fun throwing snowballs,
Then it is ruined by a stupid bell.

All the fun wrecked in an instant by a bell.

Ross Dougan (13)
The Community School of Auchterarder, Auchterarder

Best Friends Since Forever

I can't remember how I met her,
She's just always been there.
Those glistening green eyes,
That happy open smile.
Her kind, gentle nature
And perfect, pretty features.
I've always known that soft, gentle voice,
Even when shouting, it makes little noise.

Years go by and she's still there,
Forever by my side.
As things get tougher, we get closer,
To separate us would be impossible.
She puts up with me, no matter what.

Her house is like a second home,
I love her family like I love my own.
The laughs we've had, too many to count,
The tears we've cried, I don't regret.
I know her as well as I know myself.

She cares for me, rids me of fears,
She's my darling angel that's always near.
Eleven years of friendship gone,

But many more to come.

Jordan Cooper (13)
The Community School of Auchterarder, Auchterarder

My Grandpa's Funeral

My mum kept saying, 'Remember the good times,'
My stomach was filled with butterflies,
I was dreading it,
And then I sat down.

I felt special with my suit on in the pew,
With my buttonhole and laced-up shoes.
All was very silent
And then it began.

My nana's eyes were like two waterfalls,
I could see that she was grieving.
I was confused
And then I started to think.

He was in a happier place now,
I felt bad because I was glad.
The sun came out
And then the day got happier.

He came down the aisle and we were silent,
I could feel his presence with me.
He is still with me
And I remember him each day.

David Curran (12)
The Community School of Auchterarder, Auchterarder

My Dog

There's that small, black bundle
Leaping and bounding,
Jumping onto my lap.

So young and healthy,
As happy and carefree
As a newborn lamb.

As the years fly by,
He gets greyer and greyer
And slower and slower.

But still his eyes glisten
As he sniffs out the rabbits
And attempts the chase.

Now, in his bed he lies
And dreams of the past
When he didn't come last.

Emma MacLaren (13)
The Community School of Auchterarder, Auchterarder

My Baby Cousin Jack

Jack smells of baby wipes
He sometimes smells of sick
Jack has bright blue eyes
And blond, curly hair

Jack is nearly one
He has just started crawling
His hair is getting curlier every day
Jack has six teeth

Jack smiles to himself all day long
His favourite toy is his rocking horse
He sits on it every day
I love my cousin Jack.

Katie Stephen (12)
The Community School of Auchterarder, Auchterarder

Primary School

My room was alive
By the sun seeking through
I felt a bit frightened
But excited too.

As today was my first day of primary
I was strapped into the back of a car
Driving through twisted roads
Soon I came towards a huge building.

I slowly crept behind my mum
Walking towards the door
I didn't know anyone
But I didn't feel alone.

Everyone lined up outside the door
In a line like soldiers
The class was as colourful as a rainbow
With bright blue chairs and gleaming, green walls.

I sat down beside a girl called Jade
Who was really friendly
We became the best of friends
Throughout my first year.

Soon it was time to say goodbye
Until another day
As my mother picked me up outside
I said in the back of the car

'I can't wait to go back tomorrow.'

Siobhán Teague (13)
The Community School of Auchterarder, Auchterarder

7th Birth Wedding

On the twenty-eighth of May, my birthday
It was my cousin's wedding day
When I was first told I was sad
I thought I would miss my seventh birthday.

I was wrong; this birthday was one of the best
I didn't miss out on any birthday treats
I still got presents, cake and a party
And a few special birthday surprises.

When we first arrived at my cousin's house
I went to their garage and helped make some goo
We threw in eggs and soap and all sorts of things
Then we stirred it and left it till after the wedding.

After the wedding, the bride and groom
While saying thank you to staff, called my name
And said happy birthday and gave me a gift
It was one of the best gifts I got that birthday.

Then back at her home she got her photo taken
And the bucket of goo went over her
And it all happened
On the twenty-eighth of May, my birthday.

Ryan Simpson (13)
The Community School of Auchterarder, Auchterarder

Our Den, Niki's Crib

My brother disappeared as he entered the deadly mist.
I followed impatiently with Jay, Lil, Ali and Stu.
We were entranced by the beauty of Niki's Crib.

It is more hypnotic than watching the sun rise on a chilled
                                    summer's morning.
It is like the moon beaming over a frozen lake.
It has more trees than the Amazon rainforest.
Its water is fresher than water from a Scottish valley high upon
                                            the hills.

We carved our names on the tallest tree we could find.
We built a bridge over the ditch.
We built more and more as time flew past, but then the
                                    darkness came.

The trees suddenly changed into murderous maniacs.
Jack Frost came by and as he left, he took the beauty of our den
                                        with him.
The lightning came and destroyed most of the Amazon trees.
The smell of pollution was in the air from the new houses
                                    getting built.

Lyndsay Boyd (12)
The Community School of Auchterarder, Auchterarder

The Girl

She is pretty dressed in little skirts
She has beautiful plaits dangling down low
Her shoes make a little tapping noise
When she is skipping to the park

She has a twinkle
And she has a shine
When the sunshine is caught in her long, plaited hair

She holds me close in her arms
She never lets go
She always keeps me by her side

Until we reach the park
Where she plays
She leaves me there
On the wooden bench

But when it's time to go
She picks me up
And says
'Come on, my sweet teddy
Let's go home.'

Holly Milne (13)
The Community School of Auchterarder, Auchterarder

The Grade Four Piano Exam

Gravel crunches as we drive down the path
Church building, sombre and imposing
The hall, large, cold and unwelcoming
Filled with white faces and trembling hands
One by one her victims take their turn
Fearful, frozen fingers tentatively tinkle
The grinning keys, which goad them into
Their first mistake
Thoughts paralysed with fear in my head
Trying to remember what my tutor said
Mouth dry, heart beating
Like a metronome
A grey voice calls out my name
It echoes endlessly around the hall
Summoning me to my doom - *Exam Room*
As I push open the door and take in the scene
She sits behind her desk
And smiles her sinister smile
I take my seat
And so it begins . . .

Matthew Gordon (13)
The Community School of Auchterarder, Auchterarder

The Secret

I can only remember this:
Lying on a hospital bed, putting on a mask
And everything going black.

Mum rushing around telling me an ambulance is coming,
My heart fills with fear,
Wondering what's happening.

Being rushed across town to hospital,
Sirens wailing like my angry little sister,
I'm very tense, very nervous and very anxious.

This is too much worry for a seven-year-old,
We get to the hospital, rushing me to a bed,
I'm told I'm staying for at least two weeks.

Some days pass and no progress is made, until
I start to cough and struggle to breathe,
Everyone's rushing to my bedside, as my chest throbs with pain.

My whole body is filled with adrenaline,
I'm told to put on a mask, I fear for my life.
The next thing I know, everything is black.

I know I had an operation, but it went wrong.
I fell into a coma and didn't look like I'd wake up.
But after three weeks I awoke completely unharmed.

When I got home, I asked what had happened,
But if my parents wouldn't tell me, it had to be bad.
I've chosen to leave it alone for the rest of my life,

Because I've come to the decision that I never want to know.

Calum Law (13)
The Community School of Auchterarder, Auchterarder

Laughing

We looked around at the people in the room
Oblivious to us, they ate the food laid out
For them and spoke almost as if they were afraid
That no one would listen.

I was not often taken to such things
But when I was, it was like a party
Yet it was a party without music
So I would bring the entertainment.

We watched as I threw the wet paper in the air
There isn't much that friends won't do for a laugh
But, as it stuck to the ceiling, we began to realise
Just what we had done.

The atmosphere was like that of a football match
When a goal is scored, but is counted as a foul
And I was the biased referee
We had really landed ourselves in it.

We did this sort of thing all the time
It was something we could never get tired of
Seven years later, it hit me
The older you get, the more you realise it

Just how little it all mattered.

Andrew Robertson (13)
The Community School of Auchterarder, Auchterarder

First Day Of School

The first day of school,
Was a whole new beginning,
It was all very new,
The start of all my learning.

At first I did not like it,
Fighting to get away,
My mum telling me to go in,
Saying it would be OK.

After lots and lots of struggling,
I finally went inside,
The rest of the class was staring,
While I still tried to hide.

I soon got more comfortable,
But still wanted to be home,
A little boy beside,
Telling me to calm it down.

People started talking to me,
I started making friends,
Not wanting to go home anymore,
Just waiting for the end.

After a long and stressful morning,
I started enjoying school,
It wasn't as bad as I thought it was
And I still enjoy it now.

Jason Clark (13)
The Community School of Auchterarder, Auchterarder

Friends

Andrew Frazer was my first friend
I met him in primary one
He was my best friend
He would help me with anything

Calum Urquhart was my first friend
When I came to Auchterarder
He was a sort of strange type
But we are still good friends

Josh Goold is my best friend
He loves playing football with me
We always have a laugh
Like a pair of cheeky monkeys

Edward McAlister is one of my good mates
Always cheerful, well, most of the time
And a go-getter with the ladies
If you know what I mean

I have lots and lots of friends
And they're all great in ways
But there are some special ones
Those I'll remember for days and days to come.

Andrew Baxter (12)
The Community School of Auchterarder, Auchterarder

The Beginning Of School

The school seemed so big and frightening,
The playground was filling with laughter and tears,
All these small children realising,
This is where they will spend the next seven years.

Going up to the building, feeling very nervous,
And the bag on my back was weighing a tonne,
Feeling sick now, but then seeing my friends,
That feeling isn't half as bad when you know someone.

The bell screaming out, pupils piling into school,
A big blue sea of jumpers passing through,
Running into the classroom, rushing to a window,
Searching the car park for my parents to wave to.

Settling us down, the teacher giving us seats,
She sits me at a table with strangers at both ends,
Shy, sad and solemn, all already missing home,
Watching those strangers who would soon become my friends.

Sarah Balfour (13)
The Community School of Auchterarder, Auchterarder

Moving On

Small houses can be special despite their size.
I should know, I had lived in one most of my life.
The small log fire burnt brightly to keep us warm.

Slowly the house seemed to get worse as I grew,
Having only two bedrooms meant we had to share.
Privacy was unheard of as there weren't any locks.

But then things changed when my mum met up with Sandy.
Despite our differences, we all got along.
Then slowly time passed and we made a decision.

Big houses can feel strange compared to small ones.
Any house can become a home, despite its size,
Especially when faced with a choice of rooms.

Not only my house, but my friends have grown too.
Sandy's kids are here on weekends, it could be worse,
Despite their size, they can still be a lot of fun.

Although it is scary, everyone has to move on.

Hamish Maguire (13)
The Community School of Auchterarder, Auchterarder

The Giant Redwood In The Universe

The giant redwood, tall and proud
Your leafy boughs tallest in the world.
Your trunk is as thick as an elephant,
But the universe is all around,
Shrouds the tops in gentle mist,
Swamping every being.

Ben Nevis, lord surveyor of all it sees,
Is in turn downsized by the great height, Mount Everest,
Lord of all mountains.

The great tall stalks of bamboo felled by tiny ants,
The ants work hard to gather food,
Every day a battle occurs,
A great, black spider charges in,
A force of ants repel it,
Their home is safe once more.

The tiny ant is even bigger than others,
It dwarfs the atom,
But they are the most important,
Without them, nothing could exist.

The great redwood, Ben Nevis, Mount Everest, the bamboo,
Would not be here, even the tiny ant,
The bravest of them all.

James Balfour (12)
The Edinburgh Academy, Edinburgh

Pens

Pens
Felt-tip pens
Colourful, felt-tip pens
Big, colourful felt-tip pens
Standing in a circle like Stonehenge.

Joseph Doyle (13)
The Edinburgh Academy, Edinburgh

My School!

A structure of grandeur it is,
Too spectacular to be missed.

A wonder to the naked eye,
Hindering every passer-by.

This place spells 'opportunity',
Layered with a content community.

With different people of every kind,
Each and every one with a beautiful mind.

Endless joy and eternal happiness,
The best place to be, I must confess.

Amazing pupils renowned for their brain,
Who, in their life, won glory and fame!

In this castle the pen is mightier than the sword,
We bellow our success in absolute full accord!

Worth its weight in gold,
Even though it's fairly old.

An outstanding history to back it up,
In ameur propeur we raise our cups!

With intellectual teachers of unreachable calibre,
Yes! They're right here in the heart of Edinburgh!

A vast selection of subjects to learn,
For working hard, in later life we'll earn.

Michael Scott (12)
The Edinburgh Academy, Edinburgh

Sherbet Sweet

The wrapper is gleaming, it's saying 'eat me, I don't mind'.
As solid as a rock.
As sparkly as rain hitting the ground.
As good as a fresh orange.
As good as a bunch of sweets.

Sandy Campbell (11)
The Edinburgh Academy, Edinburgh

The Fairground

I heard the zoom as the clattering roller coaster swished past.
I could hear the popping of the popcorn and the whispering of
the candyfloss
And dads' faces turn green after being on the rumbling Elevator.

The splash of the white water ride
And the clang of the metal barriers letting people in and out.
Then I realised I had spent all my time in a queue for one
rubbish ride,
I guess that's the downside of the fair.

Tom Mullen (11)
The Edinburgh Academy, Edinburgh

The Seaside

I can hear the squawking of the seagulls
Kiddies crying over measles
Swimmers splashing
Children dashing
I can hear the queuing for the ice cream truck
Children running in the muck
Nobody's complaining
Cos it's not raining.

Connor Turner (11)
The Edinburgh Academy, Edinburgh

Seaside Poem

I arrived at the beach
And I could smell the lovely smell of the sea salt
As I walked down to the water.
I felt the sand surrounding my ankles.
I saw the waves crashing down and in the distance
I could hear the seagulls screeching.

Stanley Buttimore (12)
The Edinburgh Academy, Edinburgh

Koala

As grey as a stone, as soft as cotton
Crawling in the branches, eating leaves

Claws as sharp as knives, as slow as a snail
Sleeping in a trance

As hot as the sun, chomping on leaves, climbing
To new heights to find the perfect leaf
And to find the perfect bed
Australia, their home.

Jack Mackinnon (11)
The Edinburgh Academy, Edinburgh

Seaside Poem

The seagulls were howling in the wind
While the waves were crashing and the children splashing
An old man was sleeping while his child was weeping
Saying, *'I scream for ice cream!'*
He woke up in shock
While his wife was wearing a frock
So the child got his ice cream
And it was a chocolate supreme.

Colin Steedman (11)
The Edinburgh Academy, Edinburgh

My Kitten

As cute as some puppy eyes staring at you
And as it crawls up the sofa
Jumping on you
Its claws dig in
Like getting stabbed by a knife
My kitten is my special delight.

Rory Simpson (11)
The Edinburgh Academy, Edinburgh

The Seaside

I can hear
The swishing of the sea
The crashing of the waves
The crunching of the stones and shells
The squawking of the seagull

I can see
The white frothy spray of the waves
The sunrays glistening on the water
The people diving off the boardwalks
The crabs scuttling across the sand

I can feel
The sea lapping around my feet
The softness of the sand
The breeze blowing gently against my face
The slimy seaweed on my toes.

Andrew Scott (11)
The Edinburgh Academy, Edinburgh

The Night Before School

My stomach pumped with butterflies,
As my mind drifts,
Tomorrow, my future lies,
Like falling off some cliffs.

Dreaming of those metal gates,
While waiting for dawn,
Lying on my bed as my heart inflates,
Sitting on my bed, feeling as if I was just born.

Alex Brock (11)
The Edinburgh Academy, Edinburgh

Young Writers Information

We hope you have enjoyed reading this book - and that you will continue to enjoy it in the coming years.

If you like reading and writing poetry drop us a line, or give us a call, and we'll send you a free information pack.

Alternatively if you would like to order further copies of this book or any of our other titles, then please give us a call or log onto our website at www.youngwriters.co.uk

**Young Writers Information
Remus House
Coltsfoot Drive
Peterborough
PE2 9JX**

(01733) 890066